ALL ABOUT MOTORCYCLES

OTHER BOOKS BY MAX ALTH

All About Keeping Your Car Alive
All About Bikes and Bicycling
All About Locks and Locksmithing
Making Your Own Cheese and Yogurt
Plumbing

All About Motorcycles

MAX ALTH

Author of

All About Keeping Your Car Alive

HAWTHORN BOOKS, INC.

Publishers/New York

629.288   76-05959

ACKNOWLEDGMENTS

The author wishes to thank Don Santore and Richard Weir, two
veteran cyclists, for their help and encouragement in the technical
preparation of this manuscript, and especially Stewart Sillman, owner
of the Honda dealership on South Kensico Road in White Plains,
New York, a veritable nest of information and good fellowship.

Photos and drawings not credited to others are by the author.

ALL ABOUT MOTORCYCLES

Library of Congress Catalog Card Number: 74-20293
ISBN: 0-8015-0152-0

 2 3 4 5 6 7 8 9 10

To Char,
Misch,
Sime,
Sal, and
Arrabella,
without whose help I would
have finished this book months
earlier.

Contents

Preface

Motorcycling is presently second only to tennis as the most rapidly growing sport in this country. This is surprising; not that tennis is first, but that motorcycling should be second. You can play tennis with a secondhand racquet, a pair of sneakers, and some old tennis balls. There are thousands of city courts available without charge or for a small fee. Motorcycling requires at a minimum, the purchase of a cycle, and even a used machine cannot be purchased in operating condition for less than several hundred dollars. The demand is that great.

And yet people are purchasing cycles and cycling at an ever increasing rate. New clubs seem to be forming every week and new motorcycle roads and trails are being constructed by municipalities everywhere.

Why?

Cheap transportation? Possibly. Machismo—the male exhibiting his masculinity with a pair of wheels and a noisy engine? To some degree, no doubt of that. Change of pace—the motorcycle is something new? This, too, is partly the reason for the increase in motorcycling. But I don't believe any of the foregoing are the major causes, singularly or collectively.

I am convinced that the motorcycle has become popular because it has finally been recognized as an escape machine. You can do many of the same things on a bicycle, but not as quickly. On a motorized pair of wheels you are off and away from it all in a relatively short time.

Even as you are getting away from the madding crowd, you are experiencing a singular condition. With or without a companion behind you, you are, to a great degree, alone. Not the aloneness of an automobile, which many of us can drive while half asleep; but the self-contained individuality of a horseman. We don't gallop, that is true, but we can zoom and we do feel the bracing wind and the exhilaration of speed. You must guide a motorcycle, much as you do a horse, whereas at sane speeds an automobile requires almost no conscious attention.

That single facet is, I believe, the motivating force behind the surge in motorcycling that is gripping this country. The motorcycle is an escape machine and with it you can flee from a humdrum life for an hour, a day, a week, or more—something you cannot do as easily any other way.

ALL ABOUT MOTORCYCLES

1

Selecting Your Cycle

You have watched the beautiful cafe racers zip by. You have listened to the roar of massed scramblers. You have ridden jump seat behind your friend a few times. Now you want your own pair of wheels. What type, size, make of motorcycle should you start with?

GET ROAD EXPERIENCE FIRST

If you haven't driven a stick-job in traffic for a few months, do so before you attempt to ride your first motorcycle. If you have driven an automatic, that's fine, but you are still advised to get some hours on a stick-shift automobile. There is a big difference between driving an automatic and a shift transmission.

Cycles and cars have lots more in common that mere appearance might lead you to believe. Except for the Diesel-, electric-, steam-, turbine-, and rotary-powered vehicle, both cars and cycles are powered by the same cantankerous gasoline engine. Both require gears and clutches and both are shifted and clutched for the same reason—to match engine horsepower characteristics to the load. And just as important, both cycles and automobiles spend considerable time on public roads alongside other cycles and automobiles.

The gasoline engine was born with gears in its mouth. It cannot be coupled to a vehicle without clutch and gears. Some cars have automatic gearboxes and clutches. At present, cycles do not. If you take the time to learn the peculiarities of the gas engine while riding four wheels, you will not be penalized for errors. If you confine your learning to two wheels, you will get an education quite rapidly, because you will be severely punished every time you err. You can get thrown, shook up, or just plain smashed if you can't distinguish between the gas control, the brake, the gearshift, and the clutch. I can assure you that a human being's normal, noncowardly instinct is to freeze when faced by a frightening, unknown situation. In a car your instructor, supported by a second set of controls can save you. On a cycle, you are all alone.

KNOW YOUR ENEMY

If you have never driven in traffic, you can have no appreciation of just how ape some of your fellow human beings go when they get behind a steering wheel.

Those drivers who do not suffer frightening personality changes when they drive are plagued by a host of other problems and handicaps. They are absent-minded, sleepy, forgetful, stupid, inconsiderate, lacking in proper vision—they have no idea of where their car ends and your motorcycle begins—and a good percentage of them are bent on self-destruction.

It's a fact that 37 percent of all automobile fatalities required no more than one person and one car. We'll never know if the 15,000 people who died by themselves in an automobile were suicides or prey to carelessness, fatigue, drugs, and / or alcohol. And speaking of alcohol, we have nine million drunks in this country. Half the automobile fatalities last year— amounting to about 25,000 people—were killed as a result of a drunk perched behind the wheel.

You have to drive our roads a while to fully appreciate how much staying alive depends on just avoiding the other guy.

The 1974 Norton "Commando 850 Hi-Rider."
Courtesy Triumph Norton, Inc.

When you fork your first cycle and know what gas engines and road driving is all about, you can concentrate on controlling your bike. When you don't drive a stick-shift car, when you have never met a crazy automobile driver head-on, when you lack adequate traffic experience, learning everything all at once can be awfully painful.

Proof of this statement lies in the dismal fact that most cycling accidents and deaths occur during new motorcyclists' first 500 miles.

What Is Being Done with Motorcycles?

Motorcycles are being used for everything imaginable from delivering newspapers and shopping, to roaming the wilds, traveling around the world, contests, racing, and stunting at the circus and elsewhere.

In the congested cities of Europe the very small cycle—the

moped—is used by the millions for everyday transport by students, travelers, businessmen, and housewives. In this country the increasing price of gasoline has led many to use the motorcycle for commuting, making the daily train, shopping, visiting, and vacation trips. But in this country the increased use of motorcycles has occurred mostly in the general sports field. Enthusiasts are using them for camping, backwoods trail riding, cross-country trips, amateur and professional contests, and exhibitions of all varieties.

KINDS OF MOTORCYCLES

To satisfy the many applications a fair spread of basic motorcycle types has been developed over the years and many models are currently in production. Some of the motorcycle manufacturers make all types. Others confine their operation to a few. And some of the very small companies just assemble cycles, attaching their own name the way a supermarket chain sticks its own label on someone else's can of beans.

Motorcycles are manufactured in a wide variety and range of weights, speeds, power, and price. There is no simple way to group these machines. You could do it by application—trail bikes, road bikes, racing bikes. You could do it by horsepower or engine size. You could do it a number of ways, but no single way would work out neatly. Some bikes fall into two and more categories and some cyclists don't really care what kind of bike they use for what purpose.

Basic Divisions. Since the horsepower developed by a gasoline engine is directly related to its size and since bike application, to some extent, determines engine size, we can arbitrarily divide the bikes currently available by engine size. First, however, it might be advisable to review some gas engine terminology.

DISPLACEMENT

When a piston moves up and down and back up again in a cylinder, it displaces a certain amount of space. Obviously the larger the inner diameter of the cylinder, the more space is displaced. By the same measurement, the longer the piston's stroke, the more space is displaced. Simple enough.

When the piston moves down from the top of the engine, it draws in (let's not bring 2-stroke and 4-stroke engines into discussion yet) a quantity of gasoline vapor and air. The quantity is directly related to displacement. The greater the displacement, the more gas and air are sucked in and the more power developed when the gasoline / air mixture is burned.

Thus the single most important gas engine dimension is its displacement. If it is a one-lunger (single cylinder), it has the displacement of only that one cylinder. If a two-lunger, then you have the benefit of the total displacement of both cylinders.

Displacement will not give you exact or true horsepower, but the larger the displacement the more power that engine is capable of generating. The displacement is so indicative of an engine, and usually the pair of wheels to which it is attached, that most cycle makers name their cycles after the engine's displacement, plus or minus a little bit. For example, Suzuki's TS-50L Gaucho has an engine that displaces 49 cc (cc stands for cubic centimeter, and it takes 16.39 cc to equal one cubic inch). Harley-Davidson's X-90 has an engine that displaces 90.43 cc.

HORSEPOWER

Horsepower is measured in foot-pounds per minute—that is to say, the number of pounds lifted so many feet upward in one minute's time. It is based on the observed work done by large mine horses in England many years ago, and the figure is 33,000 foot-pounds per minute. The figure can be "split" any number of ways and still remain the same. For example, if you raise a one-pound weight 33,000 feet (more than six miles) in one minute, you have developed (or exerted) just 1 hp. If you life 33,000 pounds just one foot in the same time, you have developed the same power—1 hp.

A gas engine's horsepower is measured the same way, but

Suzuki's TS-50L Gaucho *Courtesy Suzuki*

SPECIFICATIONS

Length	72.0"	Horsepower	4.8 HP/8,000 rpm SAE NET
Width	32.7"		
Height	39.2"	Torque	3.26 ft.-lbs./ 7,000rpm
Wheel Base	46.7"		
Ground Clearance	7.5"	Transmission	5-speed, constant mesh
Dry Weight	156 lbs.		
Engine Type	Two-stroke, air-cooled. single-cylinder rotary valve	Tires: Front	2.50x17, 4PR Semi-knobby
		Rear	2.50x17, 4PR Semi-knobby
Bore & Stroke	1.61" x 1.49"	Fuel Tank Capacity	1.3 gals.
Displacement	49 cc		
Compression Ratio	6.7:1	Oil Tank Capacity	2.5 pts.

since it is rotating and not lifting or pulling, engine horsepower is measured in revolutions per minute (rpm) of the crankshaft and torque, which is turning power, in foot-pounds. The latter is usually measured (or given) as if at a point just one foot from the center of the crankshaft. Torque is as important as rpm (which you can visualize as speed), because rpm without accompanying torque is worthless. It is torque that actually does the pulling.

The ideal engine would be all torque and very little speed at takeoff. This is what you need to go from a standstill. Later on the ideal engine would reduce torque while increasing its rpm. The gas engine has little torque at low rpm and consequently limited power. It is not until it winds up that it develops anywhere near its rated power. What little torque it does produce is directly related to displacement. The greater the displacement, the greater the torque.

And while you can get as much hp (foot-pounds per minute from a 50-cc engine as a 100-cc engine, the smaller engine has to turn twice as fast. To use this high rpm you must gear down. The more you gear down, the more you lose in friction, and the higher the rpm at which your engine operates, the shorter its life—more turns to the mile—and the more gear changes you need from start to top speed.

Speaking of torque, I once worked on the *Sea and Bee,* a Great Lakes paddle-wheel steamer. This boat had three steam cylinders with their crankshafts fastened directly to the paddle wheels. The largest cylinder had an internal diameter of 12 feet. The engine only developed 2,000 hp (about the same as that of a prop engine on an airplane of the day). But the *Sea and Bee* would be at top speed—about 25 knots—before she fully left the dock, and it was a 500-foot boat.

2-STROKE AND 4-STROKE ENGINES

Another point to consider when selecting a motorcycle is primary engine design. There are about nine basic engine designs in use today, plus the rotary, which made its first appearance a few months ago—between Japanese wheels, of

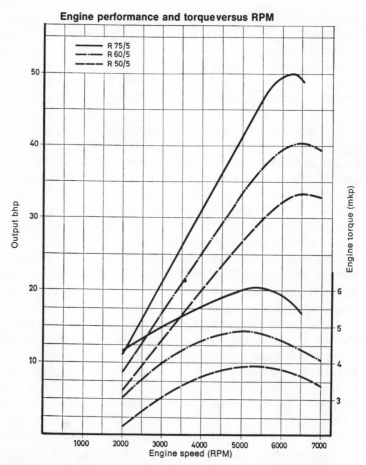

Engine performance and torque versus RPM

Typical torque versus engine rpm curves, plus a set of correlated curves providing horsepower at various rpm. (The higher curves indicate horsepower.) Each curve is for a different engine. Note that maximum hp and maximum torque do not always coincide and that torque peaks for all these engines between 5,000 and 6,000 rpm. *Courtesy BMW* course. Excluding the rotary, the nine designs can be divided into two basic types—2-strokers and 4-strokers.

Forgetting details for the moment (the engines are discussed more fully in Chapter 3), the 2-stroke or cycle engine delivers one power stroke each time the piston goes up and comes down. That is one power stroke per engine crankshaft revolution. The 4-cycle engine produces one power stroke every second time the piston goes up and comes down. That is one power stroke every two revolutions of the crankshaft. For a given piston size and a given number of engine revolutions per minute, the 2-stroke produces roughly twice as much power as the 4-stroke. It would be neat if the ratio was exactly 2 to 1. It is not, but we can accurately say that the 2-stroke produces considerably more power than the 4-stroke for the same displacement.

Because the 2-stroke engine's power strokes are closer together the effect is that of greater torque or pulling power. So why bother with the 4-cycle engine? There are several reasons.

The 4-stroke engine is essentially quieter, smoother, and longer lasting. The 2-stroke's crankshaft cannot be immersed in oil (the gas / air mixture enters through the crankcase). It is, therefore, lubricated by adding oil to the gasoline. As a result, the 2-stroke fouls more quickly and needs more attention and adjustment than the 4-stroke. One the other hand, most 2-stroke engines have fewer parts and are generally easier to service. Usually the 2-stroke engine is less costly than the 4-stroke.

Now that we have explained why it is impossible to divide motorcycles into categories, let's go ahead and do so.

MOPEDS

Their name probably stems from "motor pedaled." You start them by hopping aboard and pedaling. You can then rest your legs and let the engine pull you along a level ground, but you are expected to help out on the hills. If you don't, the engine may not make it and will stall.

Originally mopeds were nothing more than regular bicycles

with a gasoline engine fastened atop their front wheel. The Velosolex still works that way. You move a lever to lift the entire engine up and free of the front wheel. This puts the engine in neutral, so to speak, and lets it idle when you want to stand still. The system isn't neat, but it is certainly dependable. Other mopeds have their engines more or less in the conventional place between the front and rear wheels. Their frames and overall appearance resemble something between an overfed bicycle and a starved motorcycle.

Mopeds aren't beautiful but they cost under $200 new. They carry you more than 100 miles on one gallon of gas and they are useful for delivering newspapers, fetching the morning milk, and just roaming around.

Mopeds usually have no more than a 50-cc engine putting out anything from ½ to 1 hp, which isn't asking very much of the machinery and which permits moped engines to run almost forever. (For contrast, the 1974 Suzuki TS-50L displaces 49 cc and produces 4.8 net hp at 8,000 rpm.) Mopeds usually cannot do much over 30 mph, even with a strong tail wind. Therefore, some communities will not permit them on public roads. The slow-moving mopeds are considered a danger to themselves and fast-moving traffic. So check out in your neighborhood before purchasing a moped.

TRAIL BIKES

Any motorcycle operated off the road is considered a trail bike. It can even be a moped if you live out on the Great Plains and don't expect to encounter any hills. In the West and East, where hills and mountains are the norm and not the exception, trail riders usually opt for a 75-cc bike or larger. Generally it's a 2-stroke with plenty of low-gear pull to make those hills knuckle under; medium to high bottom clearance; an upswept tail pipe, and a comparatively narrow handlebar spread. A 5-speed gearbox is usually selected.

TRAIL/ROAD BIKES

Any motorcycle that performs well enough on public roads to satisfy the authorities and gives its rider a sense of security, and yet isn't so large and heavy it can't be horsed up a cliff, can be classified as a trail/road bike. Generally bikes falling into this group range in engine displacement from 125 to 150 cc.

ROAD BIKES

Any bike that has sufficient power to hold its own with public highway traffic may be classed as a road bike. Generally a 125-cc or even smaller engine is sufficient for the purpose, and usually you can get by with a 4-speed gearbox. You don't need as much low-speed pull, because you won't be climbing steep hills, and you won't need as wide a gear spread because, we assume, you won't be out with the front-running traffic.

TOURING BIKES

The difference between a road bike and a touring bike can be likened to the difference betwen a Hillman and a Rolls. They both get you there, but the tiny Hillman delivers its passengers bruised and battered from road shock and vibration, whereas the Rolls just eats up the miles with hardly a vibration. The touring bikes are the largest, heaviest, most comfortable machines made. They are big, mean, and expensive. Their engines range from 800 to more than 1,000 cc in displacement. They can weigh 700 pounds, cost more than $3,000, and deliver no more than 27 mpg in city driving. But they are comfortable.

There is also a group of smaller, lighter cycles, with 250-cc and larger engines, that are touted by their makers as touring instruments. Perhaps some drivers find them as comfortable; perhaps they are a reasonable compromise between high price, heavy weight, and comfort. Lots of them are sold, so there must be something to the ads.

RACING BIKES

Regular, organized races are held with motorcycles of almost all engine sizes. Therefore any bike is potentially a racing bike. The serious racer, however, goes to unmeasured lengths to force more power out of his cylinders than his competitors. It is done with racing cams, better cooled cylinders and heads, less restrictive air filters and exhausts, hopped up carburetion and ignition, and probably dozens of others still secret "tricks."

CAFE RACERS

This is a class of wheels that is appreciated as much for its beautiful appearance as for its speed. This writer doesn't believe many cafe racers are actually ever raced. A couple of scrambles (dirt track racing) and all the spit and polish would be ground off.

OBSERVED TRIALS BIKES

To appreciate this class of motorcycles you must first understand what observed bike trials are. They are one-man-at-a-time, observed contests over a series of fixed distances containing various types of obstacles. There will be steep turns, hills, ditches, waterholes, and other obstructions. Each contestant may walk the trial path before he tries it, but he cannot make any practice runs. Each time he touches the ground, which is called a dab, he loses one or more points. Each time he goes off course and strikes a guide tape he loses points. Whenever he is dumped he loses points. The number of points varies with each contest, and the man who loses the least points is the winner in his class.

Trials bikes usually have very small or no seats, because almost all the riding is done standing up. Their foot pegs will be farther back than usual and the fork angle will be vertical to assist the driver in making sharp turns.

A good trial bike is powerful but light, with plenty of ground clearance, knobby tires, and a heavy metal skid plate underneath the engine and transmission. The ignition will be fully waterproof and both the air intake and the exhaust will be brought up high so that the bike can traverse a stream with its rider waist-deep in the water. The trial bike engine will have a wide torque band—meaning the engine puts out that all-important pull over a wide range of rpm and doesn't peak at one particular rpm. To appreciate this statement, have a gander at the hp-torque curves for various engines.

ENDUROS

The name of this class of motorbikes comes from the name of the race, which is Enduro, meaning endurance—and that is exactly what it is all about. Generally the distance is 100 to 200 miles, and usually the race is completed in one day. However, two-day Enduros have been and perhaps still are being staged.

An Enduro is a tough run for both man and machine. The route is not as complicated, difficult, or treacherous as a trial route, but tough enough. The machines are somewhat similar. Some riders run the same rig—with perhaps a change in rear sprocket to alter the gear ratio—in both events.

Enduros are not literally races in the sense that the fastest machine wins. Instead, they are fixed-time events. The rider must reach his check points at a specific time, losing points if he gets there either too early or too late.

MOTO-CROSS

Also called a scramble, this is a closed-circuit race and is generally held on a dirt surface.

Incidentally, whatever the bike and its general or specialized purpose, bear in mind that the goal of all bike designers and manufacturers is to produce a vehicle that is strong, light in weight, and high in well-torqued power. Through the years bikes and their engines have moved in this direction. Today's bike is better than yesterday's and so on.

But if you want tomorrow's bike today, if you want a bike just a mite faster and lighter than the rest, you are going to have to pay a premium both in hard cash and in service life. Kits that increase a cycle's engine output while reducing its

Clews' CCM 4-Stroke *Courtesy Clews' Competition Machines*

SPECIFICATIONS

4-stroke engine	45 hp @ 7,000 rpm
49.8 cc displacement	Total weight 220 lbs.

weight seldom increase its life. There are exceptions—and we discuss them later on—but generally, forcing more power out of a given engine results in shortening its life.

SELECTING YOUR BIKE

If you haven't acquired at least a couple of months experience driving a stick-shift auto, if you don't know how to drive any car, if this bike is going to be your first venture into traffic on motorized wheels, start with a moped. I know it is a little like learning to bicycle with training wheels, but it is better to be a little embarrassed than to risk serious injury or death. With a little experience on the moped you can quickly and safely move on to any of the low-power, low-saddle jobs. This will enable you to plant both feet on the ground. Then you can move up in easy stages as far as you want to go. Remember, you can kill yourself quickly on a big bike if you don't know how to handle it. A big thumper can hit 50 mph in first gear and reach 60 in about six seconds. If you don't know the feel of it, it can throw you.

On the other hand, if you are past the beginner's stage and have enough common sense to take it very gently on the bigger machines, there is nothing, except money, to stop you from choosing any bike.

There is no one "best" bike. Each has its design features, advantages, disadvantages. If you are going to tool around town, you probably will want a 125-cc rig. This will be comfortable in city traffic and not too heavy to push up into the driveway. Should you wish to combine runs, perhaps a 200 or 250 cc is your meat—heavy enough for a long trip, yet light enough for city and local puttering.

As for the extras, like automatic starting and other fancy options, remember that in addition to the increased cost, there is the weight and maintenance to consider. If you select a cycle with a positive starting feature—you can kick start it in any gear—or a very clearly defined neutral, kick starting isn't much of a hassle. A couple of jumps is plenty for an engine in good condition.

WHERE TO BUY YOUR BIKE

If you are wise, you will purchase your pair of wheels from a reputable dealer near you; a dealer who has a clean, efficient, and intelligent-looking service department, a large stock room filled with parts, and a service manager who appears to know what he is talking about. Although it may sound peculiar, I'd buy the dealer not the bike. I know this makes it tough for the small guys trying to get their foot in the door, but if you do purchase an exotic wheel from a man who also sells auto-mobiles, tractors, groceries, and candy, you will probably be forced to wait months for each part you may need. The dealer near you may not have your first choice in a cycle, but he is conveniently close and he can help you. In the long run this will prove more satisfactory than the couple of hundred dollars you may have saved purchasing a bike through the mail or from a part-time dealer who may go out of business in a short period of time.

USED BIKES

There is little doubt that you can save important money by purchasing a used bike. At the same time, there is no doubt that you can also lose important money this way.

If you don't know much about bikes, it is wise to make your purchase from a reputable dealer. Make him give you a clearly written guarantee. Don't expect to save a lot of money on a used bike, but there is a saving, and it is a good way for a beginner to get started.

CHECKING OUT A USED BIKE

Evaluate its overall appearance. Is it beat, dirty? Does it look as if it has been neglected or abused? Or does it look as if the owner has taken loving care of it?

Inspect the frame for bends and dents. A shallow dent is okay, but a deep dent or a bend is NG. If any of the frame's paint looks as though heat has been applied, don't buy it. The frame was bent and later heated to straighten—the temper is gone, and the metal will be soft at that point.

Check the controls. Do they work smoothly? Check the brake and clutch for play. Note the position of the adjustments. Is there any more brake left to take up, or has it all been used? Should the latter situation be the case, you will soon need new brake shoes.

Pump the front fork up and down with a friend sitting in the saddle. The fork should move up and down slowly, indicating the shock absorber is working properly. If it bounces, the shock is kaput. It may be just lack of oil or it may be completely shot.

Try the front wheel against the handlebars. Is there any play in the bearings?

Check the wheels for centering. Spin the wheels to see if they are bent.

Check the chain. Does it feel loose in your hand? Can you bend it sideways? (Up and down is okay, but sideways indicates wear.)

Try starting the engine. Two or three jumps should do it. More may indicate maladjustment or trouble. How does it sound? How does it run? Give it a good workout. Get it really hot and try it on the hills. Any bearing knock?

Get up some modest speed and run the bike downhill. Look behind you. If you are followed by a white plume, your engine is burning oil badly.

See how the bike behaves on a smooth road with a light touch on the handlebars. It should not veer to one side. See how the bike corners—goes around a corner.

When you stop, put your finger inside the exhaust. If you find a film of oil there, the engine is using too much oil. The only sure way to cure an oil-burner is a to do a complete ring job, which usually includes reboring the cylinder(s).

If you can determine the compression of the engine—either from the bike's service manual or from the owner of a similarly aged bike in good condition—it is well worth your effort to make a compression test.

STATE LAWS

The following listing of individual state legal requirements with regard to motorcycles is current as of January 1973. It must be noted, however, that in many states legislation has already changed or is still pending concerning motorcycle activities. Prior to riding, it is advisable that the individual rider always check for any updated regulations in the states in which he will be using his motorcycle.

MOTORCYCLE REQUIREMENTS BY STATE

STATE	Special Driver License	Safety Helmet	Eye Protect.	Passenger Seat	Passenger Foot Rests	Mirror Required	Safety Inspection At Time of Reg.	Safety Inspection Periodically	Lights on all times	Handlebar 15" Ht. Limit	Riding Prohibited Two Abreast	Riding Prohibited Between Lanes	Riding Prohibited Side Saddle
Alabama	•A	•		•	•					•		•	•
Alaska	•B	•		•	•					•		•	•
Arizona	•	•	•	•	•	•				•	•	•	•
Arkansas		•	•	•	•		•	•C	•	•		•	•
California	•	•		•	•	•		•C	•D	•E		•	•
Colorado	•	•	•	•	•	•	•	•		•		•	•
Connecticut	•	•		•	•	•		•C		•	•	•	•
Delaware	•F	•	•	•	•	•	•	•		•		•	•
Florida		•	•	•	•	•	•	•	•	•		•	•
Georgia	•	•	•	•	•	•	•	•	•	•		•	•
Hawaii	•	•	•	•	•	•	•	•		•		•	•
Idaho		•		•						•			•
Illinois	•		•	•	•	•			•	•	•	•	•
Indiana		•	•	•	•			•	•	•		•	•
Iowa				•	•	•	•G			•		•	•
Kansas		•	•	•	•		•	•		•E			•
Kentucky		•		•	•	•	•	•		•			•
Louisiana	•	•		•	•	•	•	•		•		•	•
Maine	•	•		•	•		•	•		•			•
Maryland	•	•	•	•	•	•	•	•		•	•	•	•
Massachusetts	•	•	•	•	•	•	•	•		•			•
Michigan	•	•	•H	•		•		•C		•		•	•
Minnesota	•	•		•	•	•		•C		•E		•	•
Mississippi				•		•		•					•
Missouri	•	•					•	•		•			•
Montana				•	•				•	•		•	•
Nebraska		•		•	•	•	•	•		•			•
Nevada	•	•	•	•	•	•				•		•	•
New Hampshire	•	•	•	•	•					•			•
New Jersey	•	•	•	•	•	•	•			•		•	•
New Mexico	•	•I	•	•	•	•				•	•	•	•
New York	•	•	•	•	•		•	•	•	•	•	•	•
North Carolina	•	•		•	•	•	•	•	•	•			•
North Dakota	•	•	•	•	•		•			•	•	•	•
Ohio	•	•		•	•	•				•		•	•
Oklahoma	•J	•K	•	•	•	•				•L			•
Oregon	•	•		•		•		•C	•	•			•
Pennsylvania	•	•	•	•	•		•	•		•			•
Rhode Island	•	•	•	•	•	•		•		•			•
South Carolina	•	•	•	•	•	•		•	•	•	•	•	•
South Dakota	•	•	•	•	•	•		•	•	•			•
Tennessee	•	•	•	•	•	•		•		•			•
Texas	•	•				•		•		•			•
Utah	•	•M	•M	•	•		•	•		•E	•	•	•
Vermont	•	•		•	•		•	•					•
Virginia	•	•	•	•	•		•	•		•	•	•	•
Washington	•	•	•	•	•	•	•N	•C		•		•	•
West Virginia	•	•	•	•	•	•	•	•		•		•	•
Wisconsin	•	•		•	•	•		•	•	•		•	•
Wyoming		•		•	•	•	•	•C	•	•		•	•
Dist. of Col.				•	•	•	•	•		•	•		•

A. Required if under 16 years
B. Required after July 1, 1973
C. Random Vehicle Inspection
D. Required after January 1, 1975
E. Hand grips below shoulder height
F. Endorsement on license
G. First registration after sale
H. Required for speeds over 35MPH

I. Operators & Passengers under 18
J. 14-16 year-olds restricted to hours, speed and horsepower
K. Operators & Passengers under 21
L. Height limit 12 inches
M. On roads with speed limits over 35MPH
N. At time of special endorsement on license

Courtesy American Motorcycle Association, P.O. Box 141, Westerville, Ohio 43081.

Remove all the plugs and insert a standard, automotive-type compression gauge in each cylinder, in turn. With the ignition off, the gas line closed, and the throttle wide open, have a helper jump the starter a few times. The first jump will not push the gauge to its correct reading, but a few more will. If there is more than one cylinder, the compression of each should match the rest within 10 percent or so. This test is best done after the engine is thoroughly warmed up. Don't expect the engine you are testing to match other engines exactly. But if your engine's compression is 20 or more percent lower than it should be, it is probably worn and needs work.

Costs

The ticket price on a cycle is plain enough. That requires no explanation, but the hidden costs do. For example, unless you checked you wouldn't know that the insurance rates vary with the type and size cycle you purchase. The insurance on a big, fast zipper can be almost twice that of a smaller, lighter, and slower machine. You buy a bike just once, but the insurance premiums go on forever. This is something worth considering.

The cost of borrowing money is another hidden trap. If you purchase on time, your bike can cost you a third more than the bare price. If you have to borrow, get someone with heavier credit to sign the last line—someone like a father or lover. There can be considerable savings here, too. And stay away from the finance companies. Their rates run to 24 percent annually. (It's legal, but it won't hurt to complain to your congressman.) Try your credit at the bank, their rates are much lower.

2

How They Work

In the Beginning

The first self-propelled vehicle on record isn't a bicycle and it isn't a horseless carriage. It is a tricycle. Invented and constructed by a Frenchman, N. J. Cugnot, in 1769 for the French Army, it had a huge, globe-shaped copper boiler atop its single front wheel. Although one often encounters models of the forerunner of modern vehicles in museums, it could not have worked very well. There is no record of subsequent steam-powered tricycles ever being constructed.

In 1869 the Michaux Company of Paris tried a small Perreaux steam engine in one of the early bicycles of the time, as did the Copeland brothers in America. But steam engines were too heavy and necessitated lugging water and keeping the fire burning, so they didn't "take." About 1896, Humber (later of automotive fame) in England and probably others tried to power a cycle with an electric motor driven by storage batteries, but the weight of the batteries was much too great.

The idea for the first internal-combustion engine probably belongs to C. Huygens, who suggested powering an engine by exploding successive charges of gunpowder in 1690. And in

1784, one R. Street outlined an engine powered by exploding turpentine vaporized by hot metal. But it wasn't until the late 1800s that what might be termed practical, lightweight internal-combustion engines were invented and actually constructed.

N. A. Otto patented the 4-stroke engine in 1876, and in 1881, Dugald Clerk patented the 2-stroke engine. Although Clerk's name has been forgotten, the 4-stroke engine is still called the Otto cycle engine. (Incidentally, the Diesel engine was invented by a fellow actually named Diesel.)

As far as we know, Gottlieb Daimler was the first to install a gasoline engine in a cycle. The year was 1885 and his machine was practical because it was the most efficient of its time. It was a 4-stroke, single-cylinder job, displacing 264 cc, and developed ½-hp at 700 rpm—a terribly high rpm for gasoline engines of that day. His machine worked but there was no public interest, so he put it aside to work on four-wheeled carriages. His partner was a man named Benz. (Daimler-Benz makes the Mercedes-Benz auto. Mercedes is Daimler's daughter's name.)

It is difficult to ascertain who was first to manufacture motorcycles. Some credit Butler and Roots of England. Some

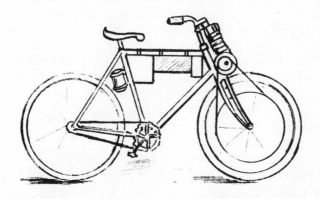

1897 Werner had an electric ignition and single-cylinder engine mounted over the front wheel. Earlier models had tube ignition and often caught fire.

give the nod to the partners Hildebrand and Wolfmuller. But no matter, by the start of this century the motorcycle was a proven fact, in commercial production and international in scope.

Of importance to ourselves at the moment is the fact that the same two engines—the 2-stroke and the 4-stroke—are still (with very small exception) powering our cycles. Basically, they haven't changed, though they have been tremendously improved.

THE 4-STROKE ENGINE

Very simply, the 4-stroke engine comprises a piston within a cylinder; the top of the cylinder mounts a spark plug and two valves. One valve acts as an exhaust valve. It extends to a tube leading to the open air. The other acts as the intake valve. It leads to the carburetor, which mixes gasoline vapor with incoming fresh air.

To operate the engine it must be started by external means. On a motorcycle the usual method is to "kick" start it. A series of gears and levers connect a pedal to the engine's crankshaft, to which the piston, connected by a rod (called piston rod) is fastened. Jumping down on the starting pedal causes the crankshaft to rotate and move the piston up and down in its cylinder.

As the piston moves up and down, the two valves open and close in sequence and in synchronization to the movement of the piston. Forgetting how synchronization is achieved for the moment, just remember that the mechanical relationship between the valves and the piston is fixed, and that the valves open and close just once for each two complete revolutions of the crankshaft. If you will, the valves operate at half the speed of the piston.

Assume the piston is moving down and the intake valve is open. This is called the intake or suction stroke. The engine draws a mixture of gasoline fumes and air into its cylinder. When the piston begins to move upward the intake valve is closed, and this stroke is called the compression stroke because the air/gas mixture is being compressed. The amount of compression is called the compression ratio.

If the internal distance from the top of the piston to the inside top of the cylinder is ten inches or cm or whatever when the piston is farthest away from the top and only one inch or cm when it is closest (This is called top dead center, TDC), the compression ratio is 9:1. If the overall cylinder space was six inches long and the piston moved five inches, the ratio would be 5:1. Most 4-stroke cycle engines have compression ratios ranging from 5:1 to 9:1.

Compressing the gas/air mixture raises its temperature, makes it easier to ignite, and helps it burn more efficiently.

The air/gas mixture is ignited by an electrical current jumping across the spark plug gap. This is called ignition and takes place about the time the piston is approaching top dead center. The instant when the plug is fired is called ignition timing, and it is synchronized with the position of the piston. Generally it is specified in degrees before TDC, and you get the degrees from the crankshaft, which, as stated, carries the piston.

The crankshaft turns on its axis. One turn is 360 degrees. If you scratch a mark on the flywheel, which is a heavy wheel attached to the crankshaft, and you carefully scribe that mark when the piston is exactly at top dead center, you know where the piston is without looking inside the cylinder. Now if you scribe more marks on the flywheel, one mark for each degree (360 all the way around), you can specify ignition at so many degrees before TDC, at TDC, or after TDC. (Keep this in mind because it is important when timing an engine's ignition.) Most engines are fired a few degrees before TDC, and with suitable (and low-cost) equipment you can adjust ignition timing while the engine is running using the marks we described.

Once the gas/air mixture is ignited it expands at a tremendous rate and drives the piston downward (away from the top of the cylinder). This is the power stroke. Both valves are closed at this time.

The piston goes down to the bottom of the cylinder and

starts upward again. At this time the exhaust valve opens and the rising piston drives the burnt gases out of the cylinder.

Obviously, this is the exhaust stroke.

There have been two complete revolutions of the crankshaft. The piston has moved most of the length of its cylinder four times—thus the name, 4-stroke or 4-cycle engine. A point to keep in mind is that all 4-strokers work exactly the same way whether the engine is in a cycle, lawnmower, racing car, airplane, or speed boat—whether there is a single cylinder or sixteen, and whether the cylinders are tiny, as in a model airplane engine, or huge, as in a truck.

4-Stroke Valves and Their Action. There are always two valves somewhere near the top end of the cylinder (opposite the crankshaft end). The intake valve is always open during the intake stroke. Intake and exhaust valves are always closed during the compression and power strokes. The exhaust valve is always open during the exhaust stroke.

Valves are "timed" in relation to the crankshaft and are usually specified in degrees, just like ignition. The intake valve opens when the crankshaft has turned so many degrees, closes after so many more degrees. Then the exhaust valve opens and closes after the elapse of a certain number of additional degrees, whereupon the crankshaft has completed two revolutions and the cycle begins all over again.

Valve timing varies with engine design. It remains fixed for the lifetime of the engine, changing a little with engine wear. Valve timing is upset or altered only when the mechanical linkage between the crankshaft and the valve-operating mechanism breaks, which rarely happens.

Cams, Rocker Arms, Push Rods. Cams are eccentrically shaped pieces of metal mounted on a revolving shaft. In some engine designs the edge of the cam rests on the end of a spring-loaded valve. As the camshaft rotates the valve is forced to move in response to the shape of the cam, which is called its profile.

The camshaft is connected to the engine's crankshaft by means of gears or a belt. The ratio between the gear or toothed pulley on the end of the camshaft and the gear or pully on the crankshaft is always 2:1. The camshaft turns just once every time the crankshaft turns twice. The valve is "timed" by relating the cam on its shaft to the position of the crankshaft. Once this is done, timing remains the same until something breaks.

Cam profile controls opening and closing time. Obviously, for maximum efficiency we want our valve to open and close quickly and to do so at the last possible second. By the same token, the sharper the curve on the cams, the more quickly they will wear and the greater the strain on the assembly. That is why stock engines are not sold equipped with "racing cams." Instead, their cams are a design compromise between maximum power and reasonable engine life.

In some engine designs the cam works against a metal rod supported by guides. The cam pushes the rod (push rod), which in turn pushes a centrally pivoted lever (rocker or rocker arm), which in turn pushes the valve. The effect is the same. There is simply more metal between the valve and its cam.

The cam arrangement for intake and exhaust valves is similar, but obviously cam profile and timing are different.

Multi-Cylinder 4-strokers. There are single-cylinder, 2-cylinder, 3-, 4-, and even 6-cylinder 4-stroke engines used on motorcycles. Although you can get as much power from a single cylinder (some giant marine Diesels produce 10,000 hp per cylinder) as you can from a number of cylinders, multi-cylinder engines offer a number of advantages and overcome some of the single cylinder's problems.

For one thing, a multi-cylinder engine is easier to start than a single-cylinder 4-stroke engine. If you have four cylinders, one cylinder will always be in the power stroke position. Thus on the average you would require one-fourth the energy to start a 4-cylinder engine and possibly half the number of revolutions. The single cylinder would have to make two turns before a power stroke came up. We are, of course, speaking of engines with equal displacements.

For another, multi-cylinder engines provide smoother power because there are more power strokes per crankshaft revolution. The multi-cylinder job is also quieter, more responsive, and has generally greater fuel efficiency per cc of displacement.

The multi-cylinder job is usually less bulky, although it may actually be a bit larger in total engine size. Crankshaft, flywheel, and associated parts can be considerably smaller on the multi-cylinder job without sacrificing strength. There is far less vibration and you have fairly steady torque instead of one big whomp every two turns.

On the other hand, the single-cylinder engine is simpler, less costly to manufacture and maintain, and very often it is lighter.

Multi-Cylinder Arrangements. The single cylinder is almost always mounted in an upright position, with the crankshaft on bottom and the plug and valves on top. Two cylinders allow for considerable variation. In some designs both cylinders are vertical and parallel. The two pistons may work alternately or in tandem. In the latter case, you have a simpler engine because both pistons move up and down together and are fired simultaneously. In some engines the two pistons on the same crankshaft work 180 degrees apart, furnishing a power stroke with every revolution of the crankshaft.

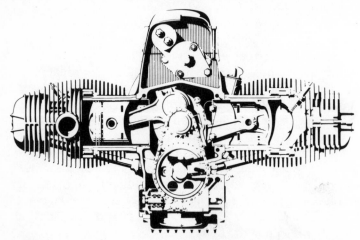

Internal view of a 4-stroke, opposed or "flat" twin engine used in the BMW S-50/5, R-60/5, and R-75/5. *Courtesy BMW*

In other arrangements the two cylinders form a V. In still others the pistons lie flat, at opposite sides of their common crankshaft. This exposes more cylinder surface to the air stream.

There are proponents of each design, and they all seem to run in and out of manufacturer's favor the way dress designs run through a department store. In any event, 4-strokers are most often described or classified by the method used to operate their valves. The more popular types are discussed in the following paragraphs.

The OHC (Overhead Camshaft)

The letters stand for overhead camshaft. In the single-cylinder configuration the usual arrangement is to mount a bevel gear on the crankshaft and use this to reduce speed and turn a larger bevel gear mounted on a vertical rod, the top end of which also carries a bevel gear. This, in turn, rotates the camshaft above the top of the cylinder. The camshaft does the usual thing and operates the two valves via two rocker arms. The overhead camshaft, single-cylinder configuration used to be very popular with racing drivers. It is rarely seen these days.

The OHV Vertical Twin

There appears to be no reason why the nomenclature should be mangled this way, but it is. An OHV vertical twin is a two-cylinder motor with both cylinders vertical, mounted side by side and attached to a common crankshaft. In place of the rotating vertical shaft there are two push rods driven by camshafts inside the crankcase and gear-driven from the crankshaft. Generally, the two pistons move up and down in their respective cylinders together, but they are fired alternately.

The OHV V-Twin

The two cylinders are set at an angle over a common crankshaft and crankcase. Both pistons move up and down simultaneously. Firing is alternate. Generally, the crankshaft has a single throw on which the big ends of the connecting rods ride between two flywheels. Push rods are actuated by a single, complex camshaft in line with the crankshaft.

THE OHV FLAT TWIN

In the configuration the two cylinders oppose one another in a horizontal plane and drive a common crankshaft. The camshaft is mounted on a gear coupled to a crankshaft gear. The rocker arms are activated by push rods. Usually each cylinder has its own carburetor, but they may draw air through a common air filter.

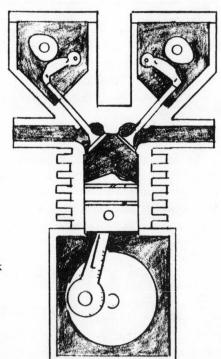

Schematic drawing of a DOHC, 4-stroke engine. Valve springs have been omitted for simplicity. Note how cams work almost directly on valve ends.

THE DOHC (DOUBLE OVERHEAD CAMSHAFT)

The letters stand for double overhead camshaft. These engines differ from the OHV's in that the camshafts are positioned above the top of the cylinder along with the valves.

There is a great mechanical advantage to this arrangement. The distance from the cam to the valve is shortened. There is less flexing and far less motion lost between the cam and the valve. Thus value action is more positive and efficient. Unfortunately, the overhead camshaft engine costs more to manufacture, and for years overhead cams were confined to expensive machines.

In operation one cam actuates the intake valve(s) and the other activates the exhaust valve(s). Both camshafts may be driven by a series of gears terminating on the crankshaft or by a chain belt also driven by the crankshaft.

So much for the basic 4-stroker. Now for the 2-stroke, which was invented a few years later. Naturally, the 2-stroke is a bit more complicated, though it has fewer moving parts.

THE 2-STROKE ENGINE

The 2-stroke differs from the 4-stroke in that the 2-stroke produces power every time the piston comes down. It differs also in the design and placement of its valves and their names. There are four valves per cylinder. One intake, one exhaust, and two transfer valves. This is basic though the valves are not always obvious and are usually called ports instead of valves.

THE PISTON-PORT, SINGLE CYLINDER

This is probably the most common 2-stroke configuration and can serve as a model for explaining how all 2-strokers work.

The top of the single cylinder is sealed except for a threaded hole that accepts the spark plug. One side of the cylinder wall has two openings or ports, one above the other. The upper port is the exhaust port and leads to the exhaust pipe and

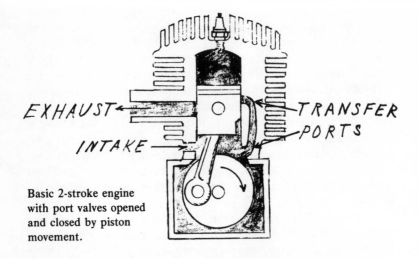

EXHAUST

INTAKE

TRANSFER
PORTS

Basic 2-stroke engine
with port valves opened
and closed by piston
movement.

through the muffler out to the open air. The lower opening is
called the intake port. This leads to a carburetor and the open
air. Let us just consider these two ports and the piston which,
of course, is connected to the conventional crankshaft.

When the piston is at the bottom of its stroke, the upper
port, exhaust, is open while the lower port, intake, is closed by
virtue of the side of the piston covering the hole. When the
piston moves up, it covers the exhaust port while uncovering
the intake port. There are two things to keep in mind here: The
lower or intake port never "sees" anything except the underside
of the piston. The upper or exhaust port never "sees" anything
except the space in the cylinder above the piston.

The two ports on the other side of the piston are called the
transfer ports. They are alternately opened (uncovered) and
closed as the piston moves up and down. Again, the upper port
communicates only with the space above the piston. The lower
port "sees" nothing more than the underside of the piston and,
of course, the crankcase. The two transfer ports are connected
by a passageway.

Now let us follow the succession of events as they occur
in more or less all standard 2-stroke engines.

Assume the piston has just passed top dead center. The fuel

charge has been ignited and the piston is moving forcibly downward under the pressure of expanding gas. First the exhaust port is uncovered and most of the expanding gas escapes. Next both transfer ports are uncovered and a gas/air mixture leaves the crankcase to enter the lower transfer port and move through the passage into the enclosed space above the top of the piston. As the piston continues to move downward, it closes the intake port. Further downward movement acts to drive more of the fuel mixture out of the crankcase and into the area above the top of the cylinder.

On the upward stroke the piston closes the exhaust port, and opens the intake port. Continued upward piston motion acts to produce a partial vacuum in the crankcase that "sucks" gas and air inside. Then the moving piston closes the transfer port and moves on to top dead center, at which time the compressed charge is fired and the cycle is repeated.

As you can see, the up-and-down motion of the piston acts to draw the fuel mixture into the crankcase. The same motion also transfers the charge from below the piston through the ports to above the piston. And once the charge is above the piston with all ports closed, continued upward motion compresses the charge.

If you have followed this explanation closely, you may have noticed that the exhaust port is open while the transfer ports are also open, at least for a fraction of the cycle. You may also wonder why the incoming charge doesn't leave with the burnt gases. Some of it does. That is why the 2-stroke is not as efficient as the 4-stroke. It doesn't give the gas mileage. Oil mileage is also comparatively poor in the 2-stroker.

The reason is that you cannot, obviously, keep the crankcase filled with lubricating oil (as in the 4-stroke) while you have the fuel charge rushing through. The oil would be quickly sucked up into the cylinder. Therefore, the 2-stroker is lubricated by mixing oil with the gasoline. The fuel charge —the air/gas mixture—carries a film of oil and lubricates all it contacts. Two-stroke lubrication is fine, but the oil in the gas fouls the cylinder much more quickly than in the 4-stroke.

Until about 1965 most cycle owners had to add a small

quantity of lubricating oil to their gasoline. Now the majority
of 2-stroke cycles have some form of automatic oil injection.
You put the lube oil into its tank and the mixing is accomplished automatically as the engine fires away.

THE PISTON-PORT TWIN

Usually the two pistons in their independent cylinders are
connected 180 degrees apart on a common crankshaft. The
cylinders are alternately fired, which makes for smoother
operation. Also, each cylinder has its own carburetor and
exhaust pipe, but ignition is supplied by a common source.

THE SPLIT-SINGLE ENGINE

This is a "kooky" kind of engine. It has only one cylinder,
but there are two pistons sharing it. In a sense, you might say
there are two parallel cylinders with a common cylinder head
and common crankcase. The connecting rods on the two
pistons join a single crankshaft, but they do not join it at the
same point. As a result, the two pistons move up and down
in a strange fashion, one alternately leading the other.

One object of the design is to keep the transfer port closed
for a longer period of time in order to improve gasoline
efficiency by reducing the quantity of gas/air rushing out of
the exhaust port. Whether or not the improved performance is
worth the complexity is not known, but this design is probably
the least used of all 2-stroke engine designs.

In any event, the split-single may be serviced just like
the standard piston-port engine. Ignition is timed according to
the manufacturer, and the pistons and rings are treated individually like ordinary pistons.

THE ROTARY-VALVE ENGINE

In this type of engine the intake port is moved from the
side of the cylinder wall to the end of the crankcase. A metal
disc with a segment cut out is mounted on the crankshaft close

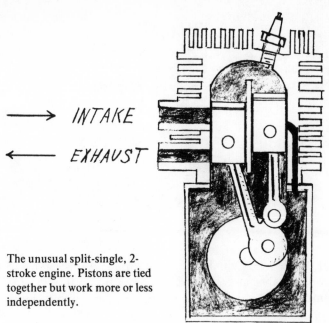

→ INTAKE

←— EXHAUST

The unusual split-single, 2-stroke engine. Pistons are tied together but work more or less independently.

to the crankcase intake port. As the crankcase rotates, the disc uncovers and covers the intake port. One side of the port is connected to the carburetor.

As the piston jogs up and down in its cylinder, it draws a fuel charge into the crankcase and then up the transfer port to the area above the piston. The rotary-valve, 2-stroke single works just like the piston-port 2-stroke single. The only difference is that intake valving is accomplished by means of a rotating disc, not by the side of the piston.

Since you can keep the intake port open or closed as long as you wish by varying the size of the missing segment, engine efficiency is improved over the piston-port engine. This is a very popular engine design, and this writer would guess that half of today's 2-strokers are of this type.

In the single-cylinder design it is usual to have the rotary valve at one end of the crankshaft, with the magneto at the

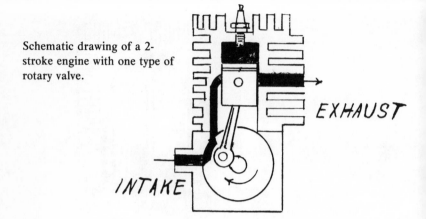

Schematic drawing of a 2-
stroke engine with one type of
rotary valve.

EXHAUST

INTAKE

other end. In the two-cylinder configuration it is customary to
have a rotary valve at each end of the crankshaft (one for
each cylinder) and to drive the magneto and points by a
separate shaft.

THE REED-VALVE ENGINE

So far we have described two methods for controlling the
incoming fuel charge on a 2-stroke engine—piston-port
valving, in which the motion of the piston covers and uncovers
the intake port, and the rotary-valve system, in which a
rotating metal disc covers and uncovers the intake port. In the
reed-valve engine the intake port is covered by a metal "flap"
that is sufficiently flexible to move in response to air pressure.

When the piston moves up and a partial vacuum is developed
inside the crankcase, the fuel charge pushes the flap to one
side and rushes in. When the piston moves down and compresses the gas/air mixture in the crankcase, the pressure developed closes the flap. Actually the valve is not a flap but a
reed—a thin flat strip of steel. In some designs there are several
reeds side by side. And sometimes the reed is called a shutter,
but the operation remains the same.

The advantage of siting the reed valve between the crank-

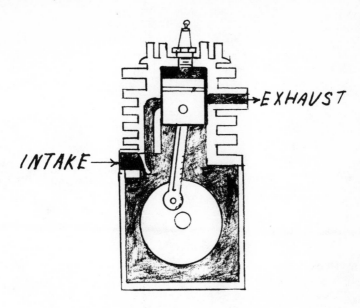

case and the carburetor over the other methods of intake valving is that there is little wear, and what wear does occur can be easily corrected by replacing the reed-valve assembly. In the case of the piston port, the wear occurs between the piston and its cylinder, which means complete reconditioning to restore original efficiency. In the case of the rotary valve, the disc can be replaced but it is difficult to reface the seat in most designs.

The reed valve is probably the single most important improvement in recent cycle engine design and is to be found in an increasing number of engines.

3

Tools

The number and type of tools you will need to keep your pair of wheels rolling along in satisfactory condition will depend on your bike and how much work you plan to do yourself.

Obviously, the more you do the more tools you will require. Not so obvious, until you purchase your cycle, is the demand each type, model, and make of cycle places on the tool box. Some bikes require several tools obtainable only from the bike maker. Others can be serviced with tools that can be purchased in a motorcycle shop or from one of the mail-order houses, a number of which are listed herewith. Other mail-order suppliers may be found listed in the various motorcycling magazines.

California Motorcycle Supply
P.O. Box 159
Fairbury, Illinois 61739

J. C. Whitney & Co.
1917–19 Archer Ave., P.O. Box 8410
Chicago, Illinois 60680

North American Imports
2325 Cerro Gordo, P.O. Box N
Mojave, California 93501

Lafayette Radio
111 Jericho Turnpike
Syosset, Long Island, New York 11791

IMPORTANT TOOLS

When I first went camping I was advised never to travel without a "possible" bag. The list of tools that follows falls into the same category. A possible bag holds everything you may possibly need. A list of must-have tools includes every essential tool.

Wrenches. Determine whether your bike has metric or SAE (standard) nuts and bolts. Although the dimensional difference between the two series of wrenches is small, they are not interchangeable. One will not fit the other. If you have metric nuts and bolts, you will find the following size wrenches most useful, especially in the 12-point design: 8, 10, 11, 12, 13, 14, 17, and 19 mm. If you have SAE nuts and bolts, you will find these sizes most useful: $\frac{3}{8}$, $\frac{7}{16}$, $\frac{9}{16}$, $\frac{5}{8}$, $\frac{11}{16}$, $\frac{3}{4}$ and $\frac{13}{16}$ inch.

Adjustable Wrench. You don't need a crescent wrench if you have the full range of open-end wrenches. But if you aren't inclined to buy open-end wrenches, the crescent wrench will do the job in most instances. However, it is important to note that some corners are too tight for an adjustable wrench.

Allen Wrenches. Sometimes called Hex wrenches, these bent, octagonal wrenches also come in metric and SAE sizes. Check this before purchasing. They come in kits, and very often the entire range of sizes costs little more than buying one or two separately.

Impact Wrench. You will need an impact wrench with a screwdriver bit to loosen some of the bike's machine screws, especially those holding the engine cover plates. These screws are installed very tightly. If you try to loosen them with a hand-driver you will rip their heads off. The impact tool keeps the driver's point in the head at the same instant the turning force is applied.

Torque Wrenches. For best results nuts and bolts should be "torqued" (tightened) to specifications. The torque value given by the bike's manufacturer assures you the nut will not loosen readily and at the same time makes certain you will not "strip" the nut's threads (rip them off). You can estimate torque to some degree by remembering that a torque of 20 foot-pounds means a pressure of 20 pounds at a distance of one foot from the center of the bolt head or nut (and so on for the other torques), but it isn't accurate by any means, especially on the lower values.

Torque wrenches come in a number of capacities and you'd do well to check your needs before making a purchase. You can't use a 0-to-50-foot-pound wrench to develop 150 foot-pounds. And you can't accurately torque a nut to 25 foot-pounds with a 0-to-150-foot-pound wrench.

Using a ratchet driver to remove a spark plug.

Using an impact wrench with a screwdriver tip to loosen a machine bolt holding the clutch cover.

Drivers. The ordinary solid-bar socket wrench driver is the least expensive type and if you don't do much work it will be more than good enough. The ratchet driver is, of course, far easier to use and much faster than the solid-bar driver. If you get one, purchase the ⅜-inch unit. The ¼-inch driver is too weak to handle the large nuts and bolts.

Vise-Grip Pliers. You can use these as a sort of third hand to hold nuts, to clamp parts together, and even as a temporary foot rest should your peg get lost.

Pliers. The old, familiar gas pliers are very useful for bending things back into shape and for tying parts up with wire when replacements parts are not available. While pliers should never be used on nuts and bolts, they can be mighty handy for other things.

Chain Breaker. A sort of vise that enables you to take a chain apart to replace a broken link (You will also need spare links and clips; without them you will have no way of repairing a broken chain.)

Screwdrivers. A six-inch and a ten-inch screwdriver with either a flat tip or a Phillips tip should handle most cycles, but some bikes need both types of tip and other need a greater variety of sizes.

Tools for the Battery

The only tool you need for your battery that hasn't been listed so far is a hydrometer. Any type will do so long as its snout is long enough to reach into all the cells.

Tools for Your Spark Plugs

You'll need a deep socket wrench—it can be an ordinary plug wrench—if you haven't purchased the proper size deep socket wrench and driver. And you will require a spark plug gauge to enable you to "gap" (adjust) the plugs.

Tire and Wheel Tools

You'll need a spoke wrench to take up slack on your wheel spokes. The ordinary, standard type is fine. The new, expensive torque spoke wrench is fine for lacing up new wheels but can lead you astray on old wheels. The reason is that you may get a false reading on a rusted spoke. It may show too high a torque while actually its tension is correct.

You will also need a pressure gauge. This is most important to tire life.

And whether you plan to fix your own flats or not, you'll be wise to include a pair of tire irons, a tube patching kit, and a couple of bottles of CO_2 along with the necessary adapter. The tire irons are very small. Tube kits for bikes include little rubber "pills" filled with rubber cement so the repair-patch equipment occupies very little space. The CO_2 bottles are only two to three inches overall and one bottle will inflate your tire sufficiently to get you home. It is a lot better than pushing your bike to a service station.

Ignition Adjustment Tools

You will need a precision feeler gauge for measuring breaker-point gap setting and one or two small wrenches for adjusting the breaker-point mechanism. To time a 2-cycle engine you'll also require a continuity tester and a timing gauge or dial indicator. To time a 4-cycle job you do not need the tester and the timing gauge. In their place a timing light and possibly a degree wheel will be necessary.

A word about ignition equipment. It isn't necessary to purchase the most expensive or complicated test equipment. In the matter of timing lights, for example, the low-cost light is as accurate as the most expensive. The only difference is in the light output. The inexpensive light is not as bright, which means you have to use it in semidarkness in order to see the light clearly.

As for the dial indicator versus the timing gauge, the dial indicator is much more convenient to use, but the gauge is sufficiently accurate.

Any continuity tester will do. It isn't necessary to have a bell ring when the light goes off. If you wish, you can easily make your own continuity tester. The diagram in the accompanying drawing illustrates how it may be done.

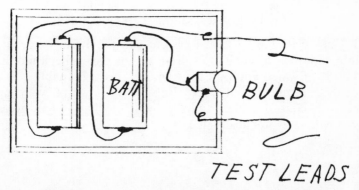

Continuity tester made of two flashlight bulbs in series with a three-volt bulb. When wire ends make contact—complete their circuit—bulb lights.

Valve Adjustment Tools

If the tappets are readily accessible, all you need is a standard set of feeler gauges. (Again check to see if your bike's manual spells it out in metric or SAE dimensions.) If the tappets are way inside, you will have to secure a special set of very long—bend around corners—feeler gauges. In addition, some wrenches will be required. In most instances, standard wrenches will do the job; In other special situations you will need a special wrench or wrenches.

Electrical System Tools and Equipment

Your best bet is a voltohmmeter, which measures voltage and electrical resistance and, therefore, can be used for a large variety of electrical tasks, including measuring generator output, coil and battery condition, continuity, and grounds.

Voltohmmeters come in a broad range of prices and qualities. I wouldn't advise the cheap three-inch kind that ranges in price from $6 to $8. It is too small to read easily and too inaccurate. I'd go for the five-inch meter that sells for about $20 at this writing. You'll find it in radio supply shops. It is sufficiently accurate for the job involved and will last for years with a little care.

Tools for General Lubrication

The single most useful tool you can purchase for general lubrication is a small pressure-type oil can—the kind that squirts oil when you pull the handle. This will enable you to easily and quickly put a few drops of oil down on your carburetor, control cables, and the like. Finally, a small grease gun will have practical value.

4

Maintenance

When I was in the army my sergeant told me on many occasions, "Take care of your gun and it will take care of you." Every time he told me this I renewed my plans for taking care of him, but the ancient homily is true enough. Your cycle is going to carry you thousands of trouble-free miles farther if you take care of it.

Establish a Program

Giving the various parts of your bike a look-see every now and again isn't a program and it certainly isn't the route to go. To make certain you do check and attend to everything at the proper time it is best to make up a list of the time or mileage intervals at which you should take care of certain maintenance or replacement functions. This may sound like a lot of fuss to write down something you are certainly going to do anyway, but it is not. Without a check list to follow, we all forget. With a guide we develop a routine that becomes automatic.

The check list that follows is only a suggestion. It isn't going to suit all cycles or all riders, but it may help you work out a suitable maintenance schedule for your bike that will keep you and your wheels safe and running for many enjoyable years to come without expensive repairs and hospital bills.

Daily Check

Check for fuel and lube oil.

Look at all the spokes.

Examine tire side walls and treads.

Sit on the bike and "eyeball" each tire to roughly check tire pressure.

Try brakes. See if they take full pressure. Check play (amount of travel before brake contacts drum or disc).

Check lights, horn, turn indicators, if any.

Check chain play (lift with your toe).

Lube drive chain.

Check play in clutch and its linkage.

Checking the tightness of the front axle nut.

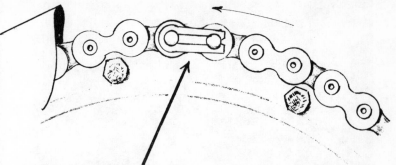

Properly positioned chain clip has closed end pointing in the direction of rotation.

Weekly Check (or Every 500 Miles)

Rap each spoke to see if any are loose.

Put a wrench on the front axle nuts to make certain they are tight.

Inspect front brake cable control and grip.

Check the front fork for play (pull back and forth on the lower end of the fork).

Check front shock absorbers. (Bounce up and down in seat. Front end of bike should move up and down slowly and not bounce.)

Check back wheel for play and centering (push wheel from side to side).

Check rear shock absorbers

Check front and rear axle nuts for tightness (put wrench to them).

Check rear brake control mechanism.

Check master link on chain (find it and see that clips fully engage pins).

Clean and lube drive chain.

Check bolts holding foot rests.

Check water level in battery.

Check battery charge.

Wipe battery top and battery enclosure clean and dry.

Remove air filter, tap on ground to clean or blow clean.

Check front wheel bearings (push wheel sideways against fork).

Check tire pressure.

Checking the front wheel assembly for play.

Monthly Check (or Every 2,000 Miles)

Remove and clean gasoline filter.
Remove and replace gearbox oil.
Change crankcase oil (4-cycle).
Check oil level at both ends of drive shaft (BMW).
Lube brake and clutch pivots and cables.
Lube twist throttle and associated linkage.
Take up slack in drive chain.
Clean engine fins.
Check steering-head bearing. (Apply front brake. Rock bike
    back and forth. Hold finger tips on bearing cap and steer-
    ing head. Movement between parts indicates loose or worn
    bearings.)
Tighten fenders, lights, horn and other attached equipment.

Every Three Months (or Every 6,000 miles)

Replace air filter.
Replace oil filter.
Replace oil in shock absorbers.
Change oil in drive shaft housing (BMW).
Lube rear swinging arm.
Inspect plug(s).
Lube centrifugal advance mechanism on breaker plate.
Check cylinder head bolt torque.
Grease or repack wheel bearings.
Grease all necessary points.
Lube breaker assembly (felt lubricator).
Check oil injection pump (2-cycle engines).
Remove cylinder head(s) and clean out carbon (2-cycle engines).
Clean carbon from muffler and exhaust pipe.
Remove chain, wash in gasoline, and relube.

5

Wheels and Tires

There is an old riddle that runs this way: Why is General Grant buried in a tomb on Riverside Drive in New York City? Few come up with the correct answer because it is so obvious. The answer is because he is dead.

Why must bike wheels and tires be given so much care? Because there are only two of them. An unexpected flat in a car can be troublesome. An unexpected flat on a cycle can be fatal. While it is obvious that there are only two wheels on a bike, there is a tendency to let wheel problems go—it's only a wheel, nothing serious. So if we belabor the point of wheel and tire care, there is good reason for it.

WHEEL CARE

Approximately every month take a wrench and give every spoke on each wheel a light rap. Each spoke should "ping," indicating it is under tension. Each ping should be of approximately the same pitch, indicating the tensions on the spokes are equal.

If a spoke is "sour" or "flat," give it no more than two full turns with your spoke wrench or any wrench that fits—you turn the nipple, of course. If two turns don't do the trick, stop right there. Remove the tube and tire and only then can you safely continue to tighten up on the spoke. If you take up on the spoke with the tire and tube in place, you will not know whether or not the spoke end is pressing against the tube. If the latter is the case, the spoke will eventually pierce the tube and will most likely blow the tube when you hit a bump right on top of that long spoke. Should a spoke project beyond the nipple, grind it off.

KEEP YOUR RIMS TRUE

Every time you need to take up more than a turn on a spoke or two it is sharp practice to see if the wheel is still "true"—meaning that the rim is still concentric with the axle (not an oval) and that the rim runs in a single plane (doesn't wobble). This is easily checked with the tires in place and the wheels on the bike.

For best results use a dial indicator (a micrometer that indicates the distance its pointer moves on a dial marked off in thousandths of an inch. For ordinary low-speed riding you can use a piece of wire and your eye. Fasten the wire to the frame and bend it so that it is close to the outside or inside of the rim's edge. Spin the wheel and keep bending the pointer closer and closer. When you have it just a hair's breadth away, spin the wheel and see if that hair's breadth varies. It shouldn't. Then move the pointer so that it almost touches the side edge of the rim. Repeat the test.

Should the wheel be out of round or wobble enough to be seen, it should be straightened. You can do this yourself, as will be explained, or have it done. A good wheel man can true a wheel to 0.003 inch both ways.

At this point you might ask, just how accurately must a wheel be trued? There isn't any specific answer, other than the higher your speed the more perfect your wheels need to be.

For a very rough test, find a big hill, put your bike in neutral, and roll down. You must reach a speed at least as high as that at which you normally ride or the test is useless.

Tap each spoke with—in this case—a spoke wrench to test for tension. Note that crossing wires have been tied together with wire for additional strength and safety.

For more accurate results, go past your normal riding speed. If you feel any vibrations at all on a smooth road with properly inflated tires, chances are one or both of your wheels are out of round, wobbly, or unbalanced (wheel balance is discussed on page 59).

Wheels can be knocked out of true (and balance) by hitting bumps, hard driving, racing, and the mere passage of time. If you have just finished a rough Trial or Enduro, or if you have bounced through a nasty pot hole and upon examination see a bent or broken spoke or a dented rim, you can be certain the wheel is warped. At the same time, it is quite possible to give the wheels a quick examination, see nothing amiss and yet have damaged wheels. So if you want to be sure, don't rely on the spoke-pinging test or eye examination alone after hitting a bump or bumps; check the wheel for true, as has been explained.

REPLACING WHEELS

Should you be planning to enter a competition or a really rugged backwoods trip, you may want to reduce your bike's weight by replacing its wheels.

Most low-priced bikes are equipped with painted or plated steel rims. If you wish, you can switch to high tensile strength steel rims, and thus increase your wheel's strength and lower its weight. For greater weight reduction you can switch to aluminum rims, with a conical hub up front. The change in hub and rim can reduce the wheel's weight by four to five pounds with no loss in strength. In fact, some riders believe the conical hubs are stronger than the regular hubs.

Since the weight you remove this way is below the springs, it is called unsprung weight and has a tremendous positive effect on bike-handling on rough roads. Some bike engineers believe each pound of unsprung weight removed is equal to the removal of ten pounds of sprung weight. Thus taking four pounds off the front wheel is equal to reducing the sprung weight by forty pounds.

CHANGING TIRE WIDTHS

If you wish to mount fatter tires or narrower tires, you can do so if the rims will accommodate the change and if there is enough clearance. The accompanying table lists the tire widths the various rims will accept without problem.

Should you want to make a tire width change greater than that which can be accepted by your present rims, you will have to change rims. An under-width (cross section) tire will slip around on the rim. An over-width tire will bulge and possibly pinch the inner tube, causing it to leak.

Before you purchase your new rims and tires, measure the

forks, make certain there is sufficient clearance to accommodate the new tire width (assuming it is larger) plus the
tire's expansion when it is a little soft and when you hit a
bump.

Following that, you must also consider the increase in overall tire height that will be produced by the new, fatter tire on
the old rim. Tire height is twice the tire cross section plus rim
diameter. For example a 3.00 x 21 tire stands 27 inches high
(3 + 3 + 21). If you were to mount a 4-inch tire on a rim of
the same diameter, the tire would stand 29 inches high
(4 + 4 + 21). The axle would be 1 inch higher from the
ground and the top of the tire would enter the forks an additional inch higher. Check to see if this increase would be a
problem before springing for new tires and rims.

Rim No.	Rim Width	Tire Cross Section
WM-0	2 inches	2.25 to 2.50
WM-1	2¼ inches	2.50 to 3.00
WM-2	2½ inches	3.25 to 3.50
WM-3	3 inches	3.50 to 4.00
WM-3.5	3½ inches	5.00 to 6.00
WM-4.00	4 inches	5.00 to 6.00

Rim size designation, rim width in inches, and range of tire cross sections (first digits in tire size) that will usually fit that rim properly.

Effect of Tire Size Change on Speed

When you switch to a larger tire and increase the effective
overall diameter on your wheel, either by using a fatter tire or
a tire with a larger diameter, you effectively increase engine-
rpm-to-rear-wheel ratio. The actual ratio remains the same.
The rear wheel (and of course this is what we are concerned
with) doesn't spin any faster but it does cover more ground
with each spin.

Therefore, to compensate for the increased ratio it is advisable to switch to a rear sprocket with one or two teeth more
than the original. This brings the effective ratio back to approximately where it was originally.

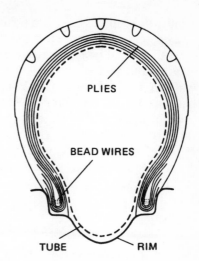

Cross section of a typical
motorcycle tire. *Courtesy
Goodyear Tire & Rubber Co.*

Switching rear wheel sizes also confuses the speedometer.
With an effectively larger diameter rear wheel you will be
moving perhaps 10 to 15 percent faster than your speedometer
indicates. (I have read that kits for correcting these errors are
for sale, but I haven't seen any in use as yet.)

HOLDING TIRES TO RIMS

In normal riding, fully inflated tires hold satisfactorily to
their rim. But to make certain and to provide tire-to-rim grip
when tires are accidentally or deliberately run soft, serrated
inner-edge rims along with tire locks or security bolts or
clamps, as they are sometimes called, are used.

These are rubber-covered metal plates fitted with central
bolts. The rubber-covered portion is placed between the inner
tube and the tire bead. The bolt goes through a hole in the
rim, just like a valve stem. The clamps are always installed in
pairs, directly opposite one another on the rim so that wheel
balance is not adversely affected. When the nut on the clamp's
bolt is run up and tightened against the rim, the clamp pulls
the tire's bead tightly against the wheel rim. Clamps work just

fine and will keep the tire from spinning on its rim and ripping the valve stem out, even when the tire is nearly flat. However, they require considerable care to install. Pinch the tube under the clamp and you've had it.

Another method requires that a number of small holes be drilled through the rim flange before the tire is installed. With the tire in place and inflated, you run some short, stainless, metal screws through the rim and into the tire. The metal screws dig into the tire's bead and prevent it from spinning under the load produced by fast getaways, jumping, and mud-chucking crawls.

TRUING A RIM ON ITS WHEEL

A true rim is concentric with its axle and is perfectly flat. That is to say, if you were to lay the rim alone on a perfectly flat surface, the entire rim's side would contact the surface. Assuming that a rim is not permanently bent, all distortion is due to improperly tightened spokes. Thus, to true a rim all one need do is adjust its spokes.

The first step is to remove the tire and tube. Remount the wheel on the cycle and lift the cycle so that the wheel can turn freely. Next, position your guide or guides so that you can readily tell when you are curing ovality and wobble.

The second step is to rap all the spokes. If one is loose, try tightening that one, then check to see if you are progressing in the correct direction. Next locate the low or high area and mark the point of greatest deviation. This is the spoke that will require the greatest amount of adjustment. The adjoining spokes will require less adjustment.

CORRECTING OVALITY

Ovality simply means egg-shaped. This dimension is controlled by the spokes going to both sides of the hub. If you have a low area—the rim is too close to the hub at that area—loosen the spokes a little at a time until it is corrected. Next tighten up on all the other spokes a little at a time. Remember, they must all "ping," meaning they must all be tensioned equally.

CORRECTING RUNOUT

Runout means wobble. This is a little confusing at first. But if you look at the wheel on end you will see that all the spokes originate in the center of the rim. Half go to one side of the hub, the balance go to the other side of the hub. Now, with the edge of the rim facing you, if you take up on the spokes going to your left hand, the rim will move to your left. If you take up on the spokes going from the center of the rim to the hub side at your right hand, the rim will move to your right.

After you have corrected runout you must go back and check for ovality and then check for equal tension, doing the

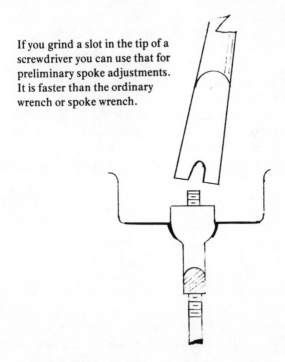

If you grind a slot in the tip of a screwdriver you can use that for preliminary spoke adjustments. It is faster than the ordinary wrench or spoke wrench.

ping bit again. Just remember that when you take up on one
set of spokes, you must ease off on the remainder; you can't
just keep tightening.

Still another point: Be advised that all rims are not equi-
distant from the sides of their hubs. If you examine some rear
wheels on edge you will see that the hub projects farther from
one side than the other. This is done to make room for gears
and the like.

LACING A RIM

The process of installing a set of spokes in a wheel is called
lacing. Lacing is more difficult than truing simply because you
have to get the "laces" in correctly before you can do your
wheel truing act.

There are nail-head and bent-head (90-degree) spokes.
There are short spokes, long spokes, stainless-steel, high-
tensile-strength steel, nickle-plated, and chrome-plated spokes.

Spoke heads used will depend on the hub design you select.
Spoke material will depend on your riding. Stainless is fine for
ordinary work. High tensile is strongest when it is nickle
plated. Chrome plating tends to make the metal brittle.

The number of spokes per wheel you need depends on rim
and hub design. The strength of the finished, laced-up wheel
depends on the type of lacing you select: zero cross, single,
double, triple, or quadruple cross. The length of the spokes you
require depends on rim and hub size *and your method of
lacing*.

LACING PATTERNS

If you have no front wheel brake and you wish to hold
weight down, zero cross is the lacing pattern for you. Each
spoke follows a radial line from hub to rim.

If you require a front wheel brake or if you are lacing a
rear wheel, you must go single or more across. In the single-
cross pattern each spoke crosses another on its way to the
rim. In the double pattern, each spoke crosses over two. In the

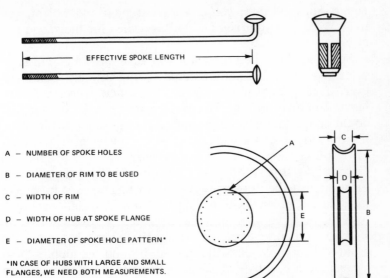

A – NUMBER OF SPOKE HOLES

B – DIAMETER OF RIM TO BE USED

C – WIDTH OF RIM

D – WIDTH OF HUB AT SPOKE FLANGE

E – DIAMETER OF SPOKE HOLE PATTERN*

*IN CASE OF HUBS WITH LARGE AND SMALL
FLANGES, WE NEED BOTH MEASUREMENTS.

How spokes are measured and the data a spoke supplier requires to select the proper spokes for your wheel. Don't forget to mention which lacing plan you are going to use. *Courtesy North American Imports, Inc.*

triple, each spoke crosses three, and in the quadruple pattern each spoke crosses four spokes.

The more spokes each spoke crosses, the longer each spoke must be and the heavier the wheel will be—but it will also be stronger.

There is nothing difficult about any of the cross patterns if you have a correctly laced wheel in front of you as a guide. Without a guide you can go clear out of your calabash. So borrow a friend's wheel before you start.

PURCHASING SPOKES

Spokes come in a number of thicknesses called gauges. The usual run varies from 6 through 10 gauge. The lower numbered spokes are thicker, heavier, and stronger. In selecting a gauge, not only must you consider strength and weight, you must be certain your rim and hub is drilled for the gauge you desire.

Spoke length is no problem if you have the old one in hand or can measure the length required on an existing wheel. However, if you are planning to lace up a new wheel and rim, length can be confusing. The easy way out is to let the supplier do the computation. Send the data suggested in the accompanying drawing, plus the method of lacing (how many crosses) to your bike shop, or to North American Imports, 2325 Cerro Gordo, P.O. Box N, Mojave, California 93501 (the company that supplied the drawing). At this writing, spokes from 3½ to 11 inches in length, 6 to 10 gauge, run 25 to 60 cents each with nipple.

After you have laced and trued the wheel, be certain to grind off any spoke ends that project beyond the nipples. And always use a new flap when the old one is worn, torn, or rust covered.

This wheel is laced one across. *Courtesy Goodyear Tire & Rubber Co.*

KEEP YOUR WHEELS BALANCED

An ounce or so of wheel unbalance builds up to many pounds when the wheel is rotating. The higher the speed, the greater the force developed. Not only does this constant pounding beat the heck out of your machine, it makes driving dangerous, because to some degree the wheel lifts when the extra weight is moving upward.

If you ride at moderate speeds along back trails, you can have the wheels balanced statically. The wheel is placed on a sensitive pivot and weights are added until it remains perfectly horizontal. If you run more than 30 or 35 mph, it is best to have the wheels dynamically balanced. In this method the wheel is spun at high speed.

You can purchase a wheel belancer of the static type for under $20, but the other type is much too expensive for just your set of wheels.

To hold the wheel in balance, do not adjust the spokes, and should you have a flat, mark the tire so that you can return it to its exact original position.

TIRES

There are three basic bike tire treads or patterns and lots of variations. The three are: street, off-the-road, and combination. The street tread has the least corrugations and indentations. Some street tires have nothing but circumferential grooves. The off-the-road tires have nothing but bumps. These are called knobby tires. The combination tire is a compromise between the first two types mentioned.

The street tire will give you the most mileage per tire. It has the most rubber on the ground and will give you the best grip in wet weather. The knobby tire will give you the least mileage. It will run comparatively hot on concrete and will, therefore, wear very fast. It will not give you maximum grip on wet concrete or even dry concrete. However, the off-the-road tire will pull you out of mud and sand up to your ankles, whereas the street tire will just spin and spin. The combination tire will give you some of the best qualities of each of the extreme designs.

Tire choice is as simple as that. However, since there are hundreds of different treads, each manufacturer and each rider touts his own. This is understandable, but don't expect any one tread design to provide maximum road and maximum muck performance. That kind of a tire hasn't been built yet.

As for the "best" tire, nylon thread or cords are still the strongest, though rayon isn't too far behind. There is no way for a rider to judge rubber quality. You can do no more than put your money down and take your chances. Just remember that the heaviest tire is the one that usually lasts the longest and is most difficult to puncture.

PLIES AND PLY RATINGS

Originally a tire was constructed of a number of layers of canvas, impregnated with rubber. Each layer was and is called

STREET   COMBINATION   OFF THE ROAD

Three basic tire tread designs. *Courtesy Goodyear Tire & Rubber Co.*

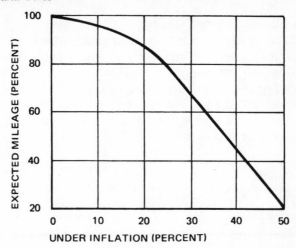

How underinflation shortens tire life. *Courtesy Goodyear Tire & Rubber Co.*

a ply. Today we have tires made of two plies that are rated 4-ply. Each ply is now twice as strong as before. Surprisingly, perhaps, an honest 4-ply rated tire is better than the actual 4-ply tire it replaces. The reason is that the two plies conduct heat out of the tire much better than the four thinner plies, and heat destroys rubber.

Tire Care

The most important thing you can do for your tires is keep them properly inflated. A soft tire drags and cuts down your gas mileage, but more important a soft tire runs hot and, as stated, it is heat that shortens tire life. An accompanying graph illustrates how much tire life you lose when you run your tires underinflated.

Low tire pressure also reduces tire-to-rim adhesion. Remember, it is the tire's air pressure that holds it in place. Run the tire soft enough and it will slide off the rim.

On the other hand, don't run them too hard. Under such conditions the tire loses traction and tends to slip. You'll get more mileage and much more tire life, but it is a dangerous practice.

The actual pressure you require will depend on your tire and the load you are carrying. The greater the weight on the wheels, the higher tire pressure you should carry. These data should be in your bike manual. If not, check with your bike dealer. Typical tire pressures, measured with the tire cold, for two popular tire sizes are given in an accompanying table. These are only ball park numbers, so it is best to get the exact figure for your pair of wheels.

Inflation Pressure (psi)	Tire Load Limits at Various Cold Inflation Pressures (lbs.)	
	3.50 x 18	4.00 x 18
12	270	340
14	300	380
16	320	410
18	350	440
20	370	470
22	390	490
24	410	520
26	430	540
28	450	570
30	470	590
32	490	610

Relation between tire pressure and load carrying ability. If, for example, your bike weighs 700 pounds completely loaded with yourself and a friend aboard, you need at least 18 psi if you are running on 3.50 x 18's. (According to the table, maximum load per tire for that tire size and load and tire pressure is 350 pounds.)

Courtesy Goodyear Tire & Rubber Co.

CHANGING TIRES, FIXING FLATS

A bike tire is similar to an automobile tire. It is removed and replaced the same way. You need two tire irons and possibly a rubber mallet, if you haven't a strong enough fist.

The tube's valve is unscrewed using a metal valve-stem cap. One tire iron is slipped under the tire's bead and the other side of the tire is compressed and pushed into the "well" in the rim. The bead is then carefully lifted up and over the edge or lip of the rim. This section is held in place with the iron. Now the second iron is slipped under the tire bead and more bead is lifted up and over the lip of the rim. If you can, you now force the rest of the bead up and over the rim. If not, you remove the first tire iron and use that to pry the bead up and over.

With one bead completely free of the rim you can remove the inner tube if you wish. If you know where the hole is and can reach the spot, you can patch the tube as it lies there.

To remove the tube and tire the second bead must be lifted up and over its rim. Obviously, to remove tube and tire the wheel must be off the bike. For a patch, this isn't always necessary.

To patch a tube, the area surrounding the hole is cleaned off and roughened with a knife edge (or the scraper in the patch kit). A thin coat of rubber cement is applied and permitted to dry. Then the cover on the patch is peeled off and the patch pressed firmly onto the rubber cement. That does it. The tube is ready to be reinflated. If there is a hole in the carcass of the tire, you can use one of the tire plugs. It looks somewhat like a huge black rubber tack. The tip goes through the hole, the balance of the patch is rubber cemented in place.

A word of caution is in order at this point. While it is common sense to carry a repair kit on a trip, personally I would not ride on a patched tube or tire unless I was just cruising down to the corner drugstore. For any sort of riding—at any speeds over 30 mph—I would replace the tube as soon as I could, and if there was more than just a nail hole in the tire, I'd replace that, too.

SAFER TIRES

The tubed tire is just about finished on automobiles. The reason is safety and tire life. The tubeless tire runs cooler, longer, weighs less, and almost never blows out. It can self-seal small punctures and it can slow down air leakage in large punctures. Holes that would immediately flatten a tube take a comparatively long time to flatten a tubeless tire. The reason is the tubeless tire's soft inner layer of rubber.

Tubeless tires, however, cannot be used on conventional wire bike wheels. The air would leak out around the spokes. What is needed is a solid wheel, and these are now being manufactured. They are "mags," wheels of cast magnesium that can be machined true to better than 0.001 inch. They can and are being used with tubeless bike tires. The change is coming, but slowly. There are some tubeless tires presently used on a few bikes, but there is no industry-wide effort to effect the change. Part of the drag is due to the cast mag's lack of resilience. Wire wheels have a certain amount of give that cast wheels do not. Another reason for the drag is the industry's reluctance to change. When the big push to switch to tubeless tires does come, it is this writer's guess it will come from Japan, like so many new things in recent years.

6

The Electrical System

You don't need a degree in electrical engineering to make repairs and adjustments to the electrical system on a motorcycle, but you do need an understanding of the fundamentals.

Electricity, as we know it, comprises the flow of vast numbers of electrons. When the electrons flow through a conductor, which is anything that easily conducts or carries electricity—copper or aluminum, for example—two things happen. A magetic field is generated around the conductor and the conductor gets warm or hot. Both these effects are useful to us. The magnetic field is used for motors (starters) and the heat is used for lighting.

MEASURING ELECTRICITY

The number of electrons that flow past any given point is measured in amperes. The pressure that drives the electrons is measured in volts. Both these quantities are very important in understanding electricity.

Except at and near absolute zero (−460° F), all conductors resist the flow of electricity. This characteristic is called resistance and is measured in ohms.

The flow of electricity through a conductor (wire) is often likened to the flow of water through a pipe. The analogy is accurate because voltage affects the flow of electricity just as pressure affects the flow of water. The higher the pressure, the greater the flow. Resistance affects the flow of electricity the way resistance affects water flow. The greater the resistance— the smaller the pipe diameter—the less water flow for a given pressure.

Amperage, or the volume of current, is dependent upon pressure and resistance. The higher the pressure (voltage), the greater the flow of current. At the same time, the lower the resistance, the greater the flow for a given pressure or voltage.

The resistance of a wire is dependent upon the material from which it is made. Copper, for example, has half the resistance of aluminum. Resistance is also dependent on the wire's cross section. The thicker the wire, the smaller its resistance and the more current it will permit to pass—again for a given voltage. This is why the starter cable on an auto or motorcycle is thick. You need a lot of current to drive the starter.

Sources of Electricity

There are two sources of electricity on a motorcycle. They are the storage battery and the generator (or alternator). The storage battery derives its power from the action of sulfuric acid on two or more plates of dissimilar lead. The generator derives its power from the motion of a conductor in a magnetic field. A moment ago we stated that the flow of electricity through a wire produces a magnetic field. Conversely, when you move a conductor through a magnetic field, a current is generated in the conductor.

The point to bear in mind here is that the storage battery (assuming that it is charged or filled with electricity) can always provide electric current whether or not the cycle's engine is running. The generator produces current only when the engine is turning over.

The Electrical Circuit

We have described electricity as a bunch of happy electrons flowing down a wire just like drops of water flow down a pipe. While this is reasonably true, it isn't the entire picture.

Electrons always return to their point of origin. (This is an oversimplification, but it serves our purpose.) For a complete water-to-electricity analogy we must picture the water leaving a tank (battery) or a pump, flowing through a pipe, and returning to the same point with no water lost, because no electricity is ever lost. Starting at the generator (pump) or battery (tank), the electricity flows around a "circuit," returning to its point of origin.

Whereas an open-ended pipe will spew forth its water, an open-ended electrical wire will not. In other words, if the circuit is broken, if there is no circuit, no current flows. This is a very important and useful facet of electricity. It makes possible all the switches we use. A switch is merely a simple mechanical means of breaking an electrical circuit. In other words, when you open a switch you are actually breaking the circle of metal that starts at the generator or storage battery, runs through the device you wish to power electrically, and returns to the generator or battery.

Grounds

Any time there is a large, convenient lump of metal handy such as the hull of a ship, the body of a car, or the frame of a motorcycle, electrical wiring can be cut in half by the simple expedient of using the lump of metal as the return wire, or one half of the circuit. Iron does not conduct electricity nearly as well as copper or aluminum, but there is so much more of it that its resistance is actually lower.

While it is best not to use the frame of the bike (or other vehicle) as an electrical return, for any of a number of reasons some bike manufacturers do (notably the British)—at least for some circuits.

On these vehicles the grounded return circuits will consist of a wire running from the battery to a switch and then to a light. From the light the electricity will run through the bike frame and up a cable to the second terminal of the battery. Assuming there is a horn, a second wire may run from a connecting point on the first wire, to the horn button, to the horn, and back to the bike frame. The passage of two distinct currents of electricity through the same bike frame doesn't confuse the little electrons at all. Each piece of equipment will function properly so long as it receives its proper share of electrical current.

High-Resistance Joints

An open switch may be considered the ultimate in high-resistance joints. The resistance of that quarter inch or so of open space between the switch's contacts is so great that no electricity at all flows. However, in the case of joints between wires, and joints between wires and the ground, oil and dirt may slip in so that some current flows, but not enough to operate the device properly. Lights, for example, would burn dimly, if at all, with insufficient current. In some instances the connections may be loose, giving rise to intermittent operation.

Short Circuits

Frequently a short circuit is called a short or a ground. The wire is said to be grounded. What this means is that the insulated wire running from the electrical source to the device has lost its insulation and the wire itself is touching the bike's frame. Or, if there are two insulated wires making the circuit, their insulation has worn away and the conductors— the metal portions—are touching each other.

In either event, electrical current never gets to its destination. Instead it takes the short route because there is less electrical resistance between the two bare wires or the wire and the ground than through the intended device. Because the current takes the short route, the condition is called a short circuit or a short. When this occurs, current flow is high and whatever fuse is in the line will "blow" or melt open.

SERIES AND PARALLEL CIRCUITS

If you needed to connect a fuse, a switch, and a horn to a battery, you would connect them all in series. That is to say, your circuit would start at the battery, go to the fuse, then through the switch, then through the horn, and finally back to to the battery. It would be one thing after another—the circuit would be a series of components.

If you needed to connect another horn, or let us say lamp, to the same battery, you would set up another series circuit. However, the second circuit would be parallel to the first. If you wanted to connect a second lamp, you would simply connect it across the first lamp. The second lamp would be in parallel with the first. This appears to be merely nomenclature, but it is much more. It is very important that you understand the relationship.

If a short developed in the horn circuit, the battery would be drained and neither of the lights would work. If the horn button itself developed a short, the horn wouldn't stop working. On the other hand, if the wire to the horn broke, the lights wouldn't be affected one way or the other.

TESTING FOR SHORTS AND OPEN CIRCUITS

Shorts have already been explained. Generally their presence is obvious. The device doesn't work, the fuse or circuit breaker (which acts like a fuse) opens up. If the presence of the short is not obvious, open the circuit—disconnect one wire—and connect a voltameter capable of reading higher than your bike's battery voltage in *series* with the circuit. If there is a short, you will read a full twelve volts, or six if you still have a six-volt battery, on your meter.

Testing for an open circuit may be accomplished the same way. If the circuit is open, there will be no reading on the voltameter.

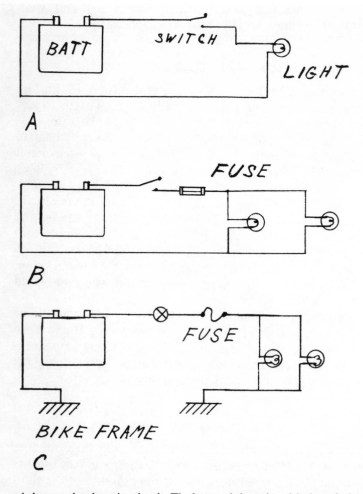

A shows a simple series circuit. The battery is in series with the switch and light. Opening the switch breaks the circuit and the light goes off.

B shows a simple parallel circuit—two lamps set up parallel with one another, and both in series with the fuse. If the fuse "blows," both lamps go out.

C shows how the bike frame is used as a "ground" or return wire. A switch has been placed in series with the fuse. The single switch controls both lamps.

If you are going to spring for a voltameter, spend a few more bucks and get a combination voltameter-ohmmeter. Or, if you prefer not to spend that much, purchase a continuity tester, which is a battery in series with a light and two test leads. Both the ohmmeter and tester are used with the bike's battery disconnected.

To use either device, connect one lead to one end of the circuit and the other lead to the other end. If the circuit is not open, the ohmmeter will show very low resistance and the light will go on. If, for example, you place your test leads across a switch, you will read "open" circuit when the switch is open and "closed" with the switch closed. Then jiggle the wires to see if any of them are loose.

Should you find the circuit open, check it out section by section. Just remember that if you are in series with a lamp you will probably get no light on the continuity tester and a reading of five to seven ohms or so on your ohmmeter.

GENERATORS

Generators on bikes are very similar to those used in automobiles, but smaller. They produce direct current, which means the electricity is always going in one direction, like that of a storage battery.

Although the output of a DC generator can be used to directly recharge a storage battery, generators aren't used very much on bikes these days (or autos either) because they are comparatively troublesome and unreliable. The difficulty stems from their commutator.

Current is generated in the heavy turns of wire wound on the laminated iron core armature, which is revolved within an intense magnetic field produced by field coils and field poles. The armature's coils are connected to a series of parallel copper bars insulated by mica. Current is taken from the copper bars, called a commutator, by two carbon brushes. As the armature rotates, the brushes wear and the armature wears. In time the mica insulation is higher than the copper and prevents proper contact. Overoiling the generator also leads to oil on the commutator—which interferes with proper current flow.

GENERATOR-STARTERS

A generator produces electrical current when it is spun. Since a generator is almost identical with a DC (direct current) motor, you can reverse the action and operate the generator as a motor by simply supplying it with electricity. This is the basis of the generator-starter motors. When the engine turns the generator's armature, current is produced. When the engine is standing still and current (from the storage battery) is fed to the same armature, it turns over and starts the engine.

In some designs the generator drives the motor through a series of step-down gears to increase the torque. When the armature is driven by the engine, the connection is direct to increase generator armature speed.

Since the generator will operate as a motor when connected to a source of current, the generator cannot be permanently connected to the storage battery. If it were, the generator would charge the battery while the bike was running, but on shutting off the engine the battery would discharge itself turning the generator (now motor) over.

To prevent this a reverse-current shut-off relay is interconnected between the generator and battery. A relay is an electrically operated switch. Generally there will be three relays in a DC charging circuit. The reverse relay can be recognized by its very heavy coil of wire. When the engine is idle, the relay is open. You can see the gap between its points (switch ends). As the engine is started and speeds up, the generator will begin to produce a voltage. When this voltage exceeds a preset value (about thirteen volts on a twelve-volt system), the reverse relay closes (the points come together), and since the generator is producing a voltage greater than that of the battery, current flows from the generator into the battery, charging it. When you cut the engine and it stops, the battery voltage starts to flow in a *reverse* direction into the generator. This energizes the heavy coil of wire and the relay is opened. Current can no longer flow into the generator and therefore, there is no battery drain.

To check the reverse relay, watch it as you increase the engine's speed from idle. Sometimes during this period it should close and promptly open up again as the engine slows down. If it doesn't close, no current is flowing out of the generator. If it doesn't open, the generator is draining the battery when the bike engine is running slowly or is stopped.

The two associate relays are both high cut-out relays. That is to say, they are normally closed but open when either current flow out of the generator is too high or voltage is too high. You will be unable to see these relays operate. They move constantly and rapidly. Note that some bikes just have two relays.

Normally these relays, called jointly the regulator, can operate for years without adjustment. But if your battery shows signs of continuous overcharging or undercharging and everything else checks out satisfactorily, have your local bike shop make the adjustments. They are tricky.

CHECKING OUT THE GENERATOR

You can rest assured your generator is putting out "something" if your headlight brightens when you accelerate your engine. However, for a more accurate determination, or to find the cause of low or no charging current, you will need a voltameter.

Start by disconnecting the thicker of the two wires connected to the generator. Connect your voltameter leads to the terminal from which the wire was removed and the generator's case. Use the twenty-volt scale for a twelve-volt system. Start the engine and watch the meter. Without a load, you ought to easily reach sixteen to eighteen volts.

If there is no voltage, disconnect the thinner wire from the generator. This is the field coil lead and may be marked Field or F. First try running a wire from the field terminal to the case of the generator and then starting your engine. If nothing results, try running a wire from the F terminal to the armature terminal, where your voltameter is connected. If there are still no results, pull the generator. There is a slight chance one of the brushes is stuck in its holder, or shattered or there is an open wire inside the case.

On the other hand, if you do develop a low voltage during these tests, don't even bother to look inside the generator case. Your best deal is to take the unit to a qualified shop, where it will be tested. Even if you do find an open or shorted field coil, you would be well advised to trade the unit in on an exchange.

MAGNETOS

A magneto is a very simple alternating-current generator. In operation it is similar to an alternator, but magnetos almost always are single-phase while alternators are usually three-phase. An alternating current is one that goes forward and backward. A single-phase alternator has one current doing this dance. A three-phase alternator has three currents doing the same thing. The three-phase is more efficient in wire and material, but the result is the same.

Typically a magneto will comprise one or more coils of wire wound on iron cores. The cores are positioned close to the engine's flywheel, which will mount several powerful permanent magnets. When the wheel rotates, the magnets pass close to the coils and the movement of the magnetic lines of force through the coils generates electrical current, just like the DC generator. In fact, a DC generator is also an alternator. It puts out DC only by virtue of the rotating switch—the commutator.

The magneto is simple. It has no rotating switch. None of the parts touch one another and it could go on almost forever if it weren't for the permanent magnets. They weaken with time and use.

When the bike has no lighting system, there will only be a high-voltage ignition circuit in the magneto. When the bike has "electricity," there will be two circuits—one for ignition and one for the battery and associated equipment.

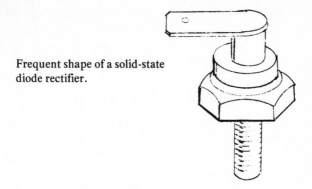

Frequent shape of a solid-state
diode rectifier.

RECTIFICATION

In order to charge the storage battery it is necessary to convert the AC current to DC. This is done by a rectifier, which is a one-way switch permitting electricity to flow through it in one direction. Some of the bikes use selenium rectifiers, and you can easily recognize them by their metal plates. Others use solid-state rectifiers, which are called diodes. They look somewhat like acorns. You can, if you wish, replace the selenium rectifier with a diode. The diode is much more efficient.

In the simpler arrangements the magneto's low-voltage coils will be permanently connected to the battery through a rectifier and usually a fuse (overload fuse). As the polarity of the battery and rectifier are such that current cannot flow out of the battery into the magneto, there is no problem (except for leakage through the rectifier).

In the more sophisticated arrangements a Zener diode may be included. A Zener is a diode that "breaks down" at a specified voltage. It is used to prevent voltage spikes from reaching the battery and to prevent the charging voltage from ever getting too high. The Zener is connected in parallel with the magneto (or alternator). So long as the applied voltage is below breakdown, the Zener does not conduct. When the voltage is exceeded, the Zener's resistance drops and the voltage is "shorted" out. On a 12-volt circuit, for example, the Zener selected would probably break down at 14.5 volts— high enough for proper charging but not so high as to cause damage; the usual consequence is to burn out the lights.

CHECKING OUT THE MAGNETO

A simple test is to watch the lights while you accelerate the engine. If there is no increase in brightness and the battery is low, chances are that the low-voltage portion of the magneto or its circuitry is at fault.

Shutting off the engine, check the diode or the rectifier by disconnecting one wire. Apply your ohmmeter across the rectifier and note its resistance. Then reverse the leads and again note the resistance. If it doesn't show at least 10,000 ohms one way and under 50 ohms or so the other way, the unit is defective. I'd replace a defective rectifier with a diode; it works better.

Diodes can be checked the same way, with the same general range of readings.

Incidentally, keep the rectifiers and diodes clean and tightly fastened to their heat sinks (metal plates). When tightening the rectifier, take care to keep the plates from turning in relation to each other.

To test a Zener, disconnect one lead, start the engine, and read the voltage across your battery. If it goes up fairly high with high engine rpm, the Zener may be okay. Connect it again, and if the voltage levels off above a fixed peak, shut off the engine again and connect your voltameter in series with the Zener. Now try her again. You should get no more than a very low voltage reading with the engine at idle and moderate speed. Then when you speed her up and exceed the breakdown voltage, you should get full magneto or alternator voltage. A high voltage at low engine rpm indicates a leaking Zener; replace it. Incidentally, Zeners get hot during normal high-engine-rpm operation.

If your magneto doesn't produce any voltage when the engine is rotating at a good clip, shut it off and check the rectifier, as described previously. Then check the Zener. It should show high resistance in both directions. If these parts pass, dismantle the magneto and check each coil for continuity. Generally the resistance of these coils is on the order of an ohm or so. Replace if any coil is open or if there is a reading when you connect your ohmmeter to one coil wire and the coil's iron core.

If the voltage output is low, and there is only one coil in the magneto, the trouble may be a short in the coil or weak magnets, neither of which can be tested with a simple, inexpensive voltohmmeter. If there are two coils and the voltage from one is low, that coil is defective. If both coils are weak, chances are the magnets are weak. Remember, a magneto produces alternating current. Unless your instrument has an AC scale (which is generally inaccurate on an inexpensive meter), you must connect your DC meter to the rectifier to get a reading. Otherwise your DC meter will vibrate and indicate zero.

ALTERNATORS

An alternator is like a magneto, because it produces AC current, and like a DC generator, because it relies on field coils rather than magnets for its magnetic flux.

Most alternators are three-phase, which means they have three coils or their armature (or stator). These coils are connected together (Y or Delta) and the AC current is delivered along three wires connected to the ends of the coils. Rectification is usually full wave, which means there are usually four diodes in the circuit.

Since your DC voltameter will not respond to AC, the only place you can measure the voltage put out by the alternator is at the wire that goes to the battery. If the voltage is low, it may be caused by one or more defective diodes. With the engine off, test them individually as discussed.

To test the field coil, check the rotor winding for continuity and grounds. (There will be two brushes and rings if the rotor is the field coil, three if it is the generating coils or armature.) To test the three-coil winding you have to open one connection between any two coils. Check for continuity and ground.

Like magnetos, alternators do not need reverse-current relays, but they do require some kind of voltage control. This may be in the form of a Zener or relay. Test as discussed previously.

Note that some motorcycles, for example the Honda 125 and 175, do not have regulators, so that it is possible to have a run-down or overcharged battery with perfectly good equipment. All you can (and should) do with such bikes is keep tabs on battery condition. If overcharged, you'd best run with your headlights on during the day. If run-down, connect a trickle charger to the battery overnight.

STORAGE BATTERIES

Storage batteries are rated in ampere hours. Thus a battery rated at 6AH (ampere hours) can, in theory, deliver six amperes for one hour or one ampere for six hours. In practice it doesn't work out quite that way. If the temperature is down to zero, the battery's capacity is reduced by about 30 percent. And in actual practice voltage falls off as current is drawn. But no matter, this is how they are rated and it is a useful guide for evaluating batteries.

Battery voltage is dependent upon the number of cells. Each cell produces about two volts. Therefore a three-cell battery provides six volts, while a six-cell provides twelve volts. Actually, the voltage will vary from eleven and a fraction to nearly thirteen according to the state of charge.

The twelve-volt battery and accompanying system is much preferred to the six because half the current is required to do the same task—blow the horn, start the engine, etc., and therefore the effect of voltage drop (resistance) in the wires and switches is halved, which means greater efficiency and power for starting and running.

Servicing the Battery. Keep a sharp eye on the level of the electrolyte (water). Do not let it fall below the tops of the plates. If it does, the exposed plate surface will dry out and your battery's capacity will be proportionately reduced. Battery capacity depends on plate area. On the other hand, do not overfill, because too much electrolyte tends to overflow the battery, and as the liquid is mild sulfuric acid it can cause considerable damage. If there are no liquid-level guides, you can figure that approximately a half inch above the plate tops is correct.

Keep the battery breather tube open and the top of the battery clean and dry. The easy way is to use some paper napkins. Moisture forms there continuously as the battery is charged. It results from the hydrogen that is released during the process. Unfortunately the hydrogen bubbles also carry drops of sulfuric acid along, so the battery top cannot be ignored.

Some riders wash the battery top down with baking soda and water, and others cover the battery terminals and cable ends with clear grease to prevent corrosion. But if any of the baking soda seeps down into the battery, you can ruin it, and the grease works its way under the battery connection. Just wiping the battery dry regularly is the best treatment.

At the same time check the battery's charge with a hydrometer. This will quickly tell you how your charging system is working. If the reading is below 1,200, your battery is low; if it is above 1,300, you are overcharging. Of the two conditions, overcharging is more serious because it will ruin a battery more quickly than chronic undercharging. Overcharging is always accompanied by rapid depletion of electrolyte.

Always use distilled water to refill your battery. You don't need much, so the cost is negligible. Tap water with a high mineral content, especially iron, will shorten your battery's useful life.

Should you need to recharge the battery from an external source, avoid a quick charge. If you have no choice, do not set it to a higher amperage rating than that of your battery.

For example, if your battery is rated at 9AH, hold the charging rate down to nine amperes. Also remove the battery from the bike and loosen the cell caps. A lot of hydrogen is released during a fast charge. You don't want pressure built up in the cells and you don't want acid mists collecting on your bike. When you replace the battery, make certain you get the polarity correct. If you reverse the battery, you can damage the diodes.

Starting Motors

All electric starting motors are alike in many ways. They are all DC operated—battery powered. All modern starters are switched on by means of a relay (starter relay), which is activated by a starter button—a press-to-make-contact switch. And all starters have a clutch system that enables the starter to

Using a "bike" hydrometer to test battery condition.

disengage the engine once the engine has "caught" and is turning under its own power.

Whether the starter works as a starter only or doubles as a generator, a few facts should be kept in mind when problems arise. First, it packs a wallop. Typically it may draw 150 amperes from a 12-volt battery, causing the battery's voltage to drop to about 8.5 volts. With this input, it is putting out about a horse and a half of physical effort. No bike battery is large enough to carry this load for more than a few seconds. So if you are having trouble starting your wheels, lay off for a few minutes between starting attempts and let the battery cool down and recover.

Troubleshooting the Starting Circuit

With the previous facts in mind, the first suspect when cranking speed is low is the battery. If it isn't up to snuff, charge it before you take anything apart.

If the battery is okay, as evidenced by the hydrometer, connect a voltameter across its terminals. Fully charged, a 12-volt battery will read about 13 volts. Now try starting the engine and watch the voltage. If it drops much below 8.5 volts, the battery has lost its capacity. It can provide the voltage but it falls off under load. Remember, we are dealing with relatively small batteries, not the brutes found in large automobiles.

If the battery is okay, look for poor connections at the bat-

Exterior view of a starting switch or solenoid. *Courtesy Suzuki*

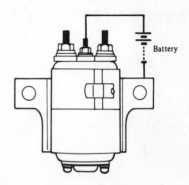

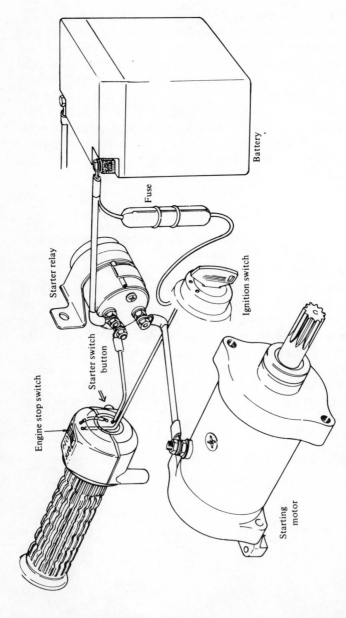

Starter relay

Engine stop switch

Starter switch
button

Fuse

Battery

Ignition switch

Starting
motor

Starting system used on Suzuki GT750. *Courtesy Suzuki*

tery posts. Remove the connectors. Sandpaper the terminal posts and the inside of the connectors clean. Try again.

The next stop is the connections to and from the starting relay, sometimes called the starting solenoid. Again, clean and tighten the connections.

If cranking speed is still low, disconnect the heavy wire from one side of the starting relay and touch it momentarily to the other heavy lead—jump the relay. If that does it, you have a worn relay, which must be replaced.

If nothing happens when you press the starting button and the battery is not way down, the trouble may lie in the starting-button circuit. Check the button and its attending wires for continuity. Then with the battery disconnected, check the starting relay coil for continuity.

The cable coming from the battery and the cable leading to the starting motor are connected to the heavy bolts and the starting switch. If they are loose, tighten them, taking care not to "ground" your wrench while you do so. The coil that activates the solenoid—the metal rod that closes the switch—will have one wire connected to a small bolt on the switch case. The other end of the coil may be connected to a second small bolt or to the metal switch case or to the large bolt connected to the cable going to the battery. Test for continuity. If open, replace.

Should your starter spin rapidly but fail to turn the engine, the clutch mechanism connecting the starter to the motor may be stuck or damaged. Disconnect the battery, then take the mechanism apart to locate the trouble.

LIGHTS AND HORN

Most bikes have a fuse in each light circuit. Some have one fuse for several lights. No matter—when the lights fail to work, check for battery power by trying the horn. If there is "battery," check the fuses. The fast test is a replacement. If you still do not have any light, try replacing the bulb. And if it's still no go, then trace the wires looking for a break.

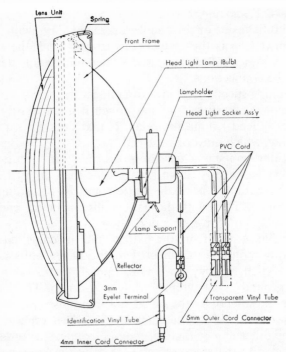

Part arrangement of a headlight. *Courtesy Honda*

Horns generally do not have any fuses in their circuits. So when they don't work, try the adjustment screw first. If this is too tight, the horn may not work. Then trace the wires and try shorting the horn button with a piece of wire or a screwdriver. If that does it, your button is at fault.

7

Ignition

The compressed charge—the mixture of gasoline and air drawn into the cylinder by the intake stroke of the piston—is ignited by an electrical spark that jumps across the spark plug gap which, of course, is the space between the center and side electrode on the engine-end of the plug.

For proper ignition the spark must be "hot," on time, and dependable. The effective temperature of the spark, its ability to "fire" the gas/air mixture, depends on the quantity of electrical current that jumps the gap. The more current, the hotter the spark. Current, in turn, depends on voltage; the higher the voltage, the greater the current and the hotter the spark. You cannot have too hot a spark, but too weak a spark results in inefficient operation, lack of power, and misfiring.

TIMING

Timing denotes the instant the spark fires, and it does its thing in microseconds, in relation to the position of the piston within its cylinder. Timing is mechanically established. So long as the parts involved do not break down, so long as no one disturbs the various adjustments, timing remains fairly constant over long periods of engine operation. With normal wear, however, timing does slow down. This means that the spark jumps the gap a fraction of a second later than it did when the mechanisms were new. Slowed spark reduces engine power.

Timing is not measured with a stop watch or any other timing device. Instead, it is measured against the position of the piston within the cylinder or the position of the crankshaft in relation to the instant of firing. In other words, timing specifications for a particular engine might read: Ignition, TDC. This means the spark is to perform its jump when the piston is as far into the cylinder as it can go, at which point the piston is at top dead center. Another engine's ignition specifications might be: 5 degrees BTDC. Interpreted, this means the piston is moving towards TDC, and proper ignition occurs when the piston's position, as indicated by the degrees of crankshaft rotation, is 5 degrees before top dead center. Thus in both examples (and all other engines) ignition would occur with the piston in a particular position, while moving in a particular direction, irrespective of engine speed. (In modern engines timing is modified by engine speed. This is discussed on page 96.)

SOURCE OF SPARK

Although 15,000 volts is sufficient to cause an electrical current to jump a half inch through air, modern cycle ignition systems develop 15,000 to 30,000 volts to make certain the current will jump the plug's gap under compression conditions.

The high voltage is produced by a transformer usually called the spark coil. The spark coil is powered by direct current supplied by the storage battery or the generator, alternator, or magneto. The spark coil (transformer) consists of two windings. The low-voltage winding consists of comparatively few turns of heavy wire over an iron core. Atop this the high-voltage coil is wound. It consists of thousands of turns of very fine wire. The step-up in voltage from the 6- or 12-volt input to the thousands of volts delivered to the plug depends on the ratio of primary turns to secondary turns. If there are a thousand turns on the secondary to each turn on the primary, the step-up in voltage will be a thousand to one.

OPERATION

As you may recall from high school physics, DC (direct current) cannot be used to power a transformer. To convert direct current to AC (actually, pulsating DC), the primary coil's circuit is opened and closed. This is accomplished with the breaker points, usually called simply points.

The current from the battery (or other source) is led though the points—which serve as a switch—and through the primary coil on the spark coil. When the points are closed, current flows into the coil. As current flows, a magnetic field is produced around the primary coil. When the points are opened, current flow stops and the field collapses. When the field abruptly collapses, a high voltage of short duration is produced in the high-voltage coil and that voltage jumps the gap in the spark plug.

The point to remember is that while a comparatively small voltage is generated in the spark coil when the points (switch)

Schematic diagram of the Honda CL72-I ignition system. Note that the stationary contact breaker arm is grounded—connected directly to the case. *Courtesy Honda*

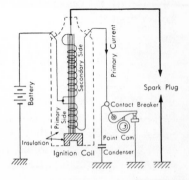

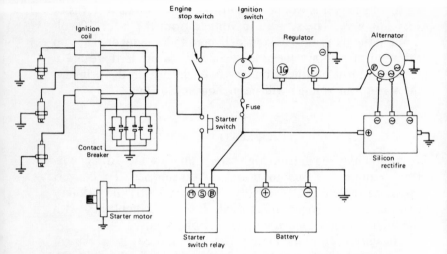

Schematic of the Suzuki GT750 electrical system including the ignition circuit. Note that there are three contact breakers and three ignition coils, one for each plug. *Courtesy Suzuki*

are closed, the big wallop is produced when the points open and current no longer flows through the spark coil's primary winding.

The collapse of the field and the consequent generation of voltage occur almost simultaneously. For all practical purposes, spark occurs when the points open, and so far as ignition timing is concerned, the opening of the breaker points is considered the instant of spark.

BREAKER POINTS

As we mentioned earlier, the plug on a 2-stroke engine is fired every time the engine's crankshaft rotates once (on a one-cylinder engine). The plug on a 4-stroke engine is fired every time the crankshaft rotates twice. To fire the 2-stroke once with every crankshaft revolution, the breaker points are operated by a cam fastened to a shaft connected directly to the end of the crankshaft (most often to an extension of the crankshaft).

Accordingly, when the crankshaft rotates, the cam opens and closes the breaker points once with every rotation. On a 4-stroke the cam operating the breaker points is connected to the crankshaft through step-down gearing so that the breaker cam turns at exactly half the speed of the 4-stroke crankshaft. Since the breaker cam is mechanically linked to the engine's crankshaft, it is obvious that the position of the cam in relation to the crankshaft and, in turn, to the piston is fixed.

When there is a single cylinder, there is only a single cam on the breaker-point camshaft. If there are two cylinders, there would be two cams or one cam with two lobes. If, for example, the cylinders operated 180 degrees apart—one piston going up while the other goes down—the two cams would be positioned 180 degrees apart. If there were four cylinders operating 90 degrees apart, there would be four cams similarly positioned on the shaft. All this holds true for 2- and 4-strokers, the only difference being the comparative speed of breaker-point camshaft rotation.

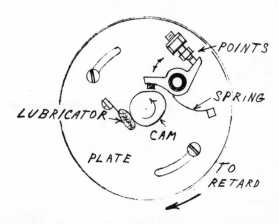

Usual single-cylinder contact breaker mounted on a plate. Note that there is only one lobe on the camshaft. Rotating plate advances or retards the spark, depending on direction of rotation.

The breaker points are usually mounted on a metal plate. One point is fixed. The other point pivots on an insulated rod. It usually has a small insulating bar that rides on the camshaft. As the camshaft rotates, the moving point swings back and forth closing and opening the ignition coil's primary (low-voltage) circuit.

Timing and Point Adjustment

All breaker points can be adjusted for timing and dwell. Timing is, as previously stated, the instant the plug is fired in relation to piston position. As manufactured, the points can be varied through a range that usually includes the correct timing somewhere at midpoint.

To vary timing, the plate supporting the points is rotated around the camshaft. If you rotate the plate against the direction of shaft rotation, you are advancing timing—ignition occurs sooner. If you rotate the plate in the same direction as the shaft rotates when the engine is running, you are retarding timing—ignition occurs that much later.

Dwell is the length of time the points remain closed. Most often this is specified in breaker-point gap, which is the distance

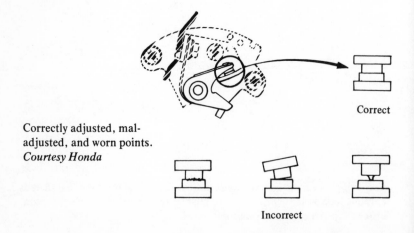

Correct

Correctly adjusted, mal-
adjusted, and worn points.
Courtesy Honda

Incorrect

the points are apart when they are most widely spaced. Dwell time is important because a sufficient interval must elapse to permit the current to fully build up in the spark coil. Collapse of the field is relatively instantaneous, but buildup is comparatively slow because of the effect of induction. Dwell time is relatively unimportant on single- and twin-cylinder engines. But it becomes increasingly important with multi-cylinder engines. No matter, even on a single-cylinder engine, dwell time specified in point gap must always be accurately set, and always before adjusting timing.

AUTOMATIC SPARK ADVANCE

It would be fine if, once ignition timing were set, it would be satisfactory for all conditions. Unfortunately, it doesn't work out that way. Let's assume that instructions call for timing to be set 5 degrees BTDC, and you do just that. If you could then connect your engine to a dynomometer and operated the engine over a range of speeds, you would find that, while efficiency might be excellent at 3,000 rpm, it wouldn't be quite as rosy at 6,000 rpm. If you located the cause, you would find (excluding other factors) that an ignition setting of 5 degrees BTDC isn't best for 6,000 rpm. At this speed, a setting of perhaps 8 degrees delivers optimum engine power. The automatic spark-advance mechanism incorporated in most cycle engines provides this change.

There are many methods used for automatically advancing the spark with increasing engine rpm. The one most often used on cycle engines is centrifugal. One or more weights revolve with the breaker-point camshaft. As the shaft's speed increases, the weight or weights move outward. The movement is coupled to the plate that holds the breaker points and the plate is rotated. While this mechanism is difficult to accurately test, you can give it a satisfactory check by trying it gently with your fingers while the engine is turned off. If it moves easily without hangup, it is okay. Just give it a few drops of oil now and again.

CAPACITOR OR CONDENSOR

When the breaker points separate and the field collapses and the high voltage fires the charge, the collapsing magnetic field also generates a fairly high voltage in the primary winding. This winding is connected to the breaker points, and as the points separate, the voltage tends to keep the arc produced there alive. In simpler terms, whereas the six or twelve volts across the breaker points ordinarily wouldn't jump the thickness of a flea's hair, the voltage developed in the primary coil can jump a considerable distance. As a result, points would be short-lived if the capacitor were not connected across them.

A capacitor is a kind of storage battery. If you connect voltage across it, current will flow into the capacitor. Remove the wires and current, or electricity remains inside—as in a storage battery. Reconnect wires to it and you can draw off the current for any desired electrical purpose.

With the capacitor across the joints during the opening or separation of the points, the moderately high voltage generated in the primary coil flows into the capacitor and very little flows (arcs) across the points. In this way point life is extended.

TESTING A CAPACITOR

Connect your ohmmeter across the capacitor, taking care to keep your fingers from touching the wires. The meter should read infinity ohms. If it indicates any resistance at all, the unit is patially shorted. Some capacitors have two leads (wires); others have only one. In the latter case connect your meter to the metal case and one lead. This test is for shorts (leakage). There is no simple, definite test you can make with your simple equipment for opens. One rough test is to short the capacitor's leads together, then try the ohmmeter. It should show a slight flick of resistance, then drift back to infinity resistance.

Since capacitors are inexpensive, if there is any doubt about proper functioning, replace. Just remember that an open

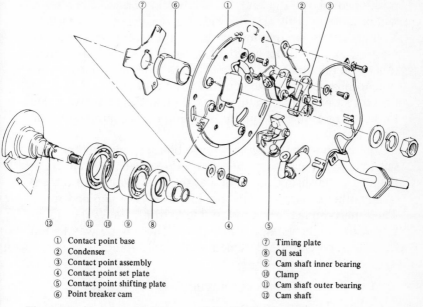

① Contact point base	⑦ Timing plate
② Condenser	⑧ Oil seal
③ Contact point assembly	⑨ Cam shaft inner bearing
④ Contact point set plate	⑩ Clamp
⑤ Contact point shifting plate	⑪ Cam shaft outer bearing
⑥ Point breaker cam	⑫ Cam shaft

Three sets of breaker points on one plate. *Courtesy Suzuki*

capacitor does not adversely affect engine operation—it merely shortens the lives of the points. A leaking capacitor reduces spark voltage. A shorted capacitor prevents a spark from being generated. In effect, with the capacitor shorted the points are always closed. If you think your capacitor is shorted, disconnect one lead and try it that way.

DISTRIBUTOR

When there is only one cylinder there is no need for a distributor because the high voltage goes to only one plug. When there are two or more cylinders a distributor (or other scheme) is needed to "distribute" the high voltage to the cylinders in proper sequence.

Forgetting other schemes and arrangements for the moment, a distributor is a rotating switch designed to handle very high voltage. Most often it is in the form of a cup or plastic cap positioned above the end of the breaker-point cam. There will be a little plastic arm that rides on the end of the camshaft. Voltage enters the distributor through a central socket in the plastic cap, travels the length of the little arm, and then jumps to a metal nib that leads to the plug. As the little arm rotates in synchronization with the camshaft, the arm always is close to the correct metal nib. In this way the high voltage is always led to the correct plug (assuming you don't mix the high-tension wires up).

There is nothing much to worry about in a distributor. Just see that it is clean, dry, and properly seated. If your rig is plagued by misfiring and poor starting and you cannot trace it to any other cause, try replacing the distributor cap and rotor. These parts sometimes develop fine hairline cracks that interfere with proper voltage distribution. There is no way to test the rotor and cap. Replacement is the only solution.

Multi-Cylinders without Distributors

To eliminate the distributor and improve high-speed performance, some bikes have individual spark coils and pairs of breaker points for each cylinder. As the camshaft rotates, it operates each set of points in proper sequence and the spark is led directly to each plug.

There are several advantages to this arrangement. As dwell time can be longer on each coil than it can be when a coil is utilized several times for each crankshaft revolution, high-rpm ignition is improved. Because less current flows through each set of points, point wear is lessened. On the other side of the coin, there are several points to adjust and replace, and the more complicated a machine, the more likely it is to fail.

As far as servicing is concerned, each pair of points and its attendant coil are treated individually. Each circuit works alone. One does not affect the other, although a shorted capacitor can prevent all of them from working.

Point Care and Adjustment

There is nothing to do to the points except occasionally place a drop of oil on the little felt or fiber lubricator that rides the cam. As the points wear, the gap between them will grow longer, retarding timing about 1 degree for each 0.001 inch of wear. At the same time the facing surfaces of the points will roughen. Don't let this trouble you. Although the surfaces pit and roughen, they still make excellent contact because one's hill is the other's valley. Once you fiddle with them, they no longer mate and contact resistance increases.

Therefore, if for some reason you have to adjust the points and their facing surfaces are not perfectly flat, *do not file the points*—replace them. If it is an emergency and you cannot replace the points, it is best not to fiddle with them. Slightly maladjusted points are far better than the results you will get trying to file them with a point file or a strip of emery paper, because it is impossible to make the tungsten points perfectly flat by hand.

Gapping the Points. To adjust the maximum distance to which the points open (separate), turn off the ignition, remove the plug(s), loosen the proper screw on the point that does not swing, then turn the engine over by hand until the high point on the cam is directly under the rubbing block and the points are wide open.

The plugs are removed to make it easier to turn the engine over by hand. Sometimes you can do this easily by turning the flywheel. In other instances you will want to place a wrench on the end of the crankshaft. It all depends on the engine.

But no matter what method you use to get the high point of the cam under the rubbing block, you must do so by turning the engine over in its normal direction of rotation. The setting may be inaccurate if you rotate the crankshaft backward to position the cam.

The next step consists of adjusting the stationary point. Usually there are two bolts. One locks the little arm, the other is an eccentric; turning this moves the arm and varies the gap. Adjust to the manufacturer's specification using a clean, non-wrinkled feeler gauge. Don't guess. The gap is critical. When adjusted, tighten up the locking screw. Turn the engine over a few times to make certain you really had the cam in the proper position.

If the points look good when you remove the cover—and you may need to refer to manufacturer's instructions to do that with many models—wash the assembly down with solvent and check the gap without loosening any of the screws. If it is close and the bike is running well, leave them alone. Place a drop of oil on the lubricator (felt pad) or a drop of grease under the rubbing block.

IGNITION TIMING

Gas engine points are set to open and fire a specified number of degrees BTDC (before top dead center) or at TDC (top dead center). The setting varies with engine design and gasoline used. High test fuel can be fired a fraction earlier than regular gas.

Basically there are two ways to time ignition—static and dynamic. You can do it with the engine standing still and you can do it with the engine running. The second method is far better. In fact, you should always check timing dynamically even though your engine's construction may be such you have to set it "cold."

LOCATING THE PISTON

As already stated, timing is related to piston position within the cylinder. Your first task is, therefore, to determine where that piston may be without taking the engine apart. If your bike maker is a kindly fellow, he has marked the crankcase and crankshaft so that all you need do is line the marks up. On some engines you will find just two marks. On others you will find a mark on the crankshaft (flywheel) and a series of degree marks on the case so that you adjust timing as many degrees BTDC as specified.

If there are no timing marks—and some compact engine designs do not permit them—you locate the piston by "feel." This is done with a dial indicator or a special micrometer (depth). The plug is removed and the engine shaft is rotated until the piston is as close to TDC as you can see or feel with

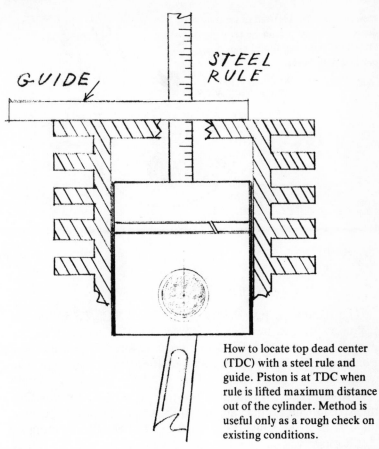

GUIDE

STEEL RULE

How to locate top dead center (TDC) with a steel rule and guide. Piston is at TDC when rule is lifted maximum distance out of the cylinder. Method is useful only as a rough check on existing conditions.

a pencil. Then the dial indicator or micrometer is used to "feel" for the very last fraction of piston height. The indicator is best because movement of its tip pressed against the top of the piston can be easily read on the dial in thousandths of an inch so you can see the piston come up to and pass TDC.

If I did not have either of the aforementioned instruments, I would use a steel rule to see if the ignition setting were close to specifications, and if so, I would leave it alone.

How degree wheel is used to set
degrees before top dead center
after TDC has been found and
marked with pointer.

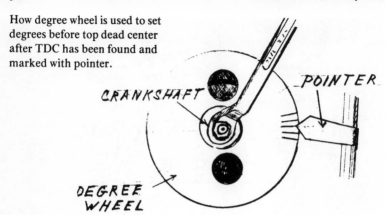

Cold BTDC Setting

The technique just described locates TDC. To locate the
piston a specified number of degrees BTDC you have two approaches. If specified, BTDC can be measured in piston travel.
For example, Yamaha specifies ignition on some models to
occur 1.8mm (0.071 inch) BTDC. To find this piston position
you would locate TDC with the indicator, note the reading,
then rotate the crankshaft and quit when the piston brought
the dial to a point just 0.071 inch short of the first reading.

Alternately, you can mount a degree wheel on the end of
the crankcase. This is a plastic or cardboard wheel marked off
in degrees. In the case of the Triumph, a degree wheel is
provided that fits under a bolt on the end of the ignition camshaft, which is also the end of the crankcase. To use this wheel
or any other wheel, you find TDC as previously discussed.
Then you stick a piece of pointed scotch tape on the exhaust
pipe or any other piece of the frame or engine with the tape's
point resting at zero on the degree dial. Now you can turn the
crankshaft and the wheel indicates just how many degrees you
have gone.

POSITIONING THE POINTS

At this stage you have properly gapped the points. Now you want to adjust them so that they open at the proper instant. You do this by rotating the plate supporting the point assembly. To make certain you know exactly when the points separate, connect a continuity tester across them. If the tester indicates on, all the time, disconnect one wire leading to the moving point. (We did say ignition off, didn't we?)

You can purchase a continuity tester or make one from a light bulb in series with a battery. Don't use an ohmmeter, as the needle movement is damped and it reacts too slowly.

With the continuity tester connected, we slowly rotate the engine's crankshaft until the points just open. This is indicated

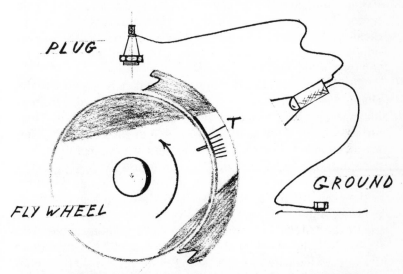

Using a timing light. Generally, if there is more than one cylinder, the lead is connected to number one plug. If light won't go on, disconnect high-tension lead from plug and connect light directly to lead. When mark on flywheel is opposite correct mark on crankcase, timing is on the nose.

by the light going out. If the points separate just as the piston reaches its correct position—TDC or BTDC—all is well. If not, loosen the plate holding the breaker-points assembly and rotate it in the required direction. Tighten the plate and turn the crankshaft again to see if you have made the proper adjustment. It is not at all difficult; it just takes a little fiddling. Just remember that the crankshaft is never backed up. It is always turned in the normal direction of rotation. When you are done, you "timed" the engine.

DYNAMIC IGNITION TIMING

If your engine has timing marks or if you can add them, you should check timing dynamically, because no matter how careful you may be with the engine off, timing is a little different with the motor running.

On some engines you can rotate the ignition plate with the motor running, which eliminates the need to fuss with dial indicators. On others, you will have to shut down before you can adjust timing. In either case, the procedure and instrument used are the same.

The instrument is a timing light, which is a gaseous discharge lamp that lights up the instant it is powered. Ordinary incandescent lamps take a little time to light and go out. There are timing lights for as little as $3. and as much as $25. They are all equally accurate. The cheap ones put out less light. You need darkness or at least deep gloom to use them.

The principle of the timing light is simple enough. The light is powered by the spark. The light flashes for a couple of microseconds—just long enough for your eye to see and retain the image (about 1/60th of a second). The moment the light flashes is the moment your crankshaft should be in its correct position as indicated by the timing mark on the shaft in relation to the mark or marks on the crankcase. If the marks line up you are in good shape; if not, you must vary timing until they are.

On some bikes you can rotate the breaker-point plate while

the engine is running. When you do this you will see the mark on the crankcase move, which makes it easy. On others you have to stop the engine to adjust the breaker plate. On some engines you can rotate the entire assembly.

MULTI-CYLINDER ENGINES

Up to this point we have ignored engines with more than one cylinder because multi-cylinder engines—2-strokes or 4-strokes—are treated almost the same.

If your engine has a set of breaker points for each cylinder, set the gaps on all of them first. Then time one pair as per specifications. Now, depending on engine design, all the breaker points may be properly timed, or each additional pair of points needs to be timed. This should be obvious when you examine the supporting plate. Whether all are timed or not, it is good practice to use the timing light to check each cylinder's timing independently.

When an engine has several cylinders (and you can now purchase bikes with as many as six cylinders), one set of breaker points, and a distributor, all you need to do is set the points for any cylinder to have all the cylinders timed properly. (Generally you adjust for cylinder one, but see your manual to be certain.)

TYPES OF IGNITION SYSTEMS

Although the general instructions given apply to almost all gas engine ignition systems, there are some variations that may puzzle you. So here is a description and some tips.

Standard Systems. The most common type of system consists of an alternator, magneto, or generator that charges a storage battery which, in turn, powers the spark coil through breaker points. Let's call this system standard.

Constant-loss ignition. To save the weight of the storage battery some competition machines omit them. In their place a fair-sized capacitor, which acts like a very small storage battery, is used. Starting is a little more difficult, but running is just as good. However, the machine is illegal on the roads of many states because it has no lights when the engine is shut off.

Servicing the ignition system of these machines is no different from servicing standard ignitions. Just bear in mind that the engine will stall if you let it idle too slowly; alternator voltage falls off.

To test the capacitor connect it across a battery, taking care to watch the polarity—plus on the capacitor to plus on the battery—and the voltage. Don't put a 6-volt capacitor across a 12-volt battery; you can blow it. Wait a moment. Remove the battery, then short the capacitor. You should see a fat, healthy spark jump across. If you have any doubts about it, try a replacement or even a storage battery. You cannot check an electrolytic capacitor with an ohmmeter. Don't forget to watch the polarity when attaching the replacement capacitor.

CD Systems. CD (capacitor discharge) ignition systems differ from standard in that the breaker points connect a capacitor to the primary ignition coil winding instead of connecting that coil directly to the storage battery. Since capacitors discharge rapidly, the resultant spark is of shorter duration but more intense. Ignition is better and the fast spark will often fire fouled plugs that would not be fired by a standard ignition system.

Transistorized Ignition. This is somewhat similar to the standard system, and in its simplest form the breaker points control a transistor which, in turn, switches current on and off through the primary winding. The advantage is that less than one-tenth the usual current flows through the points, thus greatly extending their life and reducing maintenance.

Breakerless Ignition. This is, possibly, the ultimate system. Breaker points are replaced by a small coil and a small magnet on the ignition camshaft. As the magnet passes the coil, a voltage is produced in the coil. This voltage is amplified and used to trigger the spark coil. There is no physical contact between the rotating magnet and the coil. Therefore, there is no wear, and supposedly once set at the factory a breakerless ignition system requires no further attention.

Spark Plugs

In addition to being of vital necessity to the operation of an engine, spark plugs are invaluable aids in determining engine condition, so you are advised to learn how to read them.

Plug Types and Ranges. Plugs come with various threads, in various heat ranges, and with various reaches. Thread size and plug diameter are obvious. You need an exact replacement or it's no go. Reach is something one doesn't ordinarily think about until it is too late. Reach is the depth a plug "reaches" into the cylinder. If it is too shallow, ignition suffers. If it is too deep, it can ruin the engine when the top of the piston strikes the plug's end. So always make certain the replacement plug has the proper reach. Measure it against the old.

Heat range is determined by the shape of the plug. Long, thin plug tips run hotter than the fat ones, which conduct the heat more rapidly. If your plug shows white, change to a cooler plug. If it shows black, change to a hotter plug—after everything else has been checked out. Bear in mind, however, that long runs at moderate to high speeds call for colder plugs than local riding.

Reading Plugs. When everything is working properly, the tip of the plug should be an even pale-brown or tan color. If the inside end of the plug is white, the plug is running too hot. This may be caused by a lean fuel/air mixture. The carburetor may be incorrecely set or there may be a leak at the gasket where the carburetor joins the engine or intake manifold. Another possibility is that the plug is too "hot" (see above).

If your plug is black and fouled with oil, the cause may be too "cold" a plug for your particular fuel/air mixture; too rich a mixture (too much fuel); or a crankshaft leak permitting gearcase oil to get into the crankcase (this would be a 2-stroke engine).

Also, if you have an older engine and are adding your own oil to the gasoline, you may be using too much oil proportionately; you could be using the wrong type of oil (the new synthetic 2-stroke lube oil is best); or your atuomatic oil injector is shooting too much oil.

If you are running a 4-stroke engine and the plug is carbonized, you may have too much oil in the crankcase, but more likely your rings are worn and crankcase oil is getting into the working end of the cylinder.

Removing and Replacing Plugs. Wait until the engine is at least lukewarm so you will not burn yourself. Take care to clean the plug well completely before you remove the plug. Always use a proper size plug wrench.

When replacing a plug, always clean the seat so the plug makes firm contact. Always use your fingers to start the plug. If its threads are rusty, place a few drops of oil on them. You want to be certain you aren't cross threading the plug, which you might be doing if starting was difficult. Make the plugs snug, preferably with a torque wrench to specifications. Without a torque wrench to guide you, make them snug when the block is cold. Nothing much will happen if the plug loosens up. If you overtighten the plug you can easily rip the threads right out of the head.

Gapping and Cleaning Plugs. If the central electrode is rounded or if there is a "neck" in the horizontal electrode, replace the plug. Don't waste time on it. If the coating on the plug is so hard it is almost like glass, you should replace it. If you can clean the plug in plug-cleaning solvent, fine—don't waste time and money having the plug sand-blasted clean. It's ceramic glaze is destroyed and it will not last long.

Use a wire gauge to gap the plugs. The flat strip gauge is no good for this. Gauge carefully. The plug's gap is critical.

IGNITION ACCESS

In the preceding pages the impression was possibly given that all one had to do to gain access to the ignition breaker points was to remove a cover or two. Unfortunately, this is far from true in many instances. On many bikes getting to the points is the hardest part of the job. To reach the points for inspection on the Yamaha Mini-Enduro, for example, you must first remove a cover (easy enough), but then you have to work through holes in the flywheel. To gain full access to

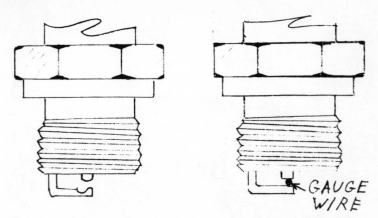

When the plug's electrodes are rounded and worn as shown at left, it is time to replace the plug. Use a wire gauge to measure plug's gap correctly.

the points you need to remove the gear lever and another cover.

To get to the Suzuki TS-250 magneto and points you must first remove the left sidecase cover. Then you need Suzuki's rotor holder #00930-40111 or a strap wrench. This is used in conjunction with Suzuki's flywheel puller #09930-30711. No other tool can be used because the flywheel is rather thin and easily damaged. Other flywheels are or become sealed to the tapered end of the crankshaft on which they ride. These flywheels require a shock puller to break them loose.

If you do not know whether or not your pair of wheels requires special tools, check with your dealer or bike manufacturer before you have a go at the ignition.

On the other hand, the ignition systems of some bikes are easily reached, as for example the Kawasaki 500CC Mach III and the BSA 650.

8

Brakes

Two types of brakes are currently used on motorcycles: internally expanding, mechanically operated drum brakes and hydraulically operated disc brakes.

Both types are similar to their automotive counterparts. Motorcycle mechanically operated drum brakes work just the way the mechanical brakes used on cars in the 1920s did. They are also repaired and adjusted the same way. The same is also true of motorcycle hydraulically operated disc brakes and disc brakes on modern cars. Sizes and shapes are somewhat different, but if you know how car brakes operate, you'll have no problem with motorcycle brakes.

Two Types of Drum Brakes

When you squeeze the brake lever on the handlebars of a motorcycle, the end of the lever pulls on a cable which, in turn, pulls on a second lever attached to a rod. The rod carries a cam—an oval-shaped piece of metal. When the rod turns, the cam turns and spreads two semicircular brake "shoes." These push against the inside of the brake drum, and the fric-

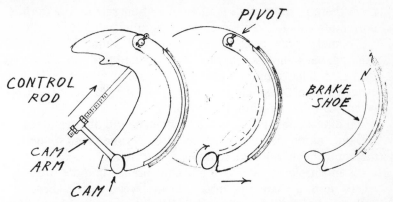

Major parts of the mechanical drum brake. When control rod (or cable) is moved in the direction shown, cam on arm turns, spreading the brake shoes apart. When cam goes too far, as shown at right, it gets stuck and will not return to its normal position. Brake remains "on."

tion between the shoes and the drum stops the latter from rotating.

This type or design is called the single-cam brake. Since both shoes are pivoted at one end and are spread at their other end by the rotation of the cam, the free end of one shoe points toward the direction of drum rotation. The other free end points away from the direction of rotation.

Assume for a moment that you are grinding a point on a chisel with the help of a power-driven grindstone. You know from experience that you must position the metal so that the wheel turns away from you. If you position the metal so that the wheel turns toward you, the point of the chisel will catch and be driven toward yourself.

Getting back to the two brake shoes, the shoe that is pointing in the direction of drum rotation is called self-energizing. It tends to lock itself against the drum. The other shoe merely presses against the inside of the drum. Its braking effectiveness is much lower.

Single-cam brakes are often chosen for trail riding because it is very often necessary to brake to prevent oneself from rolling backward down a steep hill. With the single-cam arrangement there is always one leading or self-energizing brake shoe no matter which direction the bike is moving.

To make both brake shoes inside the drum "lead" when braking, each shoe is independently pivoted and moved by its own cam. The result is a brake that is about 50 percent more effective than the single-cam brake, but it is far less effective when the bike is rolling backward.

To differentiate between the single-cam and dual-cam brake without taking them apart, inspect the brake drum's side. If the control cable or rod (coming from the foot brake) terminates in one lever, it is a single-cam brake. If there are two levers, it is a dual-cam brake. Both levers move when the brake is operated. Don't mistake the torque rod or bar for a brake lever. The torque bar fastens the brake plate to the bike's frame. Without it the brake-shoe assembly would rotate with the wheel when the brake was applied.

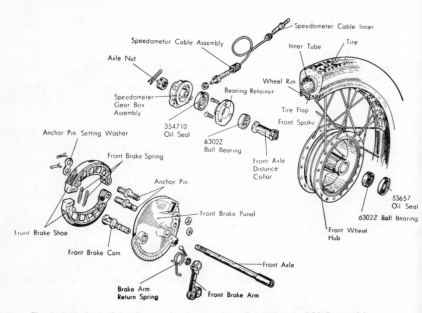

Exploded view of the front wheel assembly of the Honda 250 Scrambler.
Courtesy Honda

ADJUSTING MECHANICAL BRAKES

When to Adjust. In the normal course of riding and stopping brakes wear slowly and fairly evenly. As they do, control lever (hand) and pedal (foot) strokes becomes longer and longer. When the brakes are new and correctly adjusted there will be about ¾ inch of "play" in the controls. When the stroke reaches about 1½ inches, adjustment is necessary. This will vary from cycle to cycle, but it is an approximate and useful guide.

There is no need to make the adjustment more frequently. On the other hand, you do not want to delay until you find that you have no brake. This condition can occur when the controls reach their natural stops—end of their stroke—as well as when the brake shoes wear out completely.

Primary Adjustment. You'll find a ferrule (nut) followed by a standard nut at the end of the hand control lever brake cable. Loosen the normal nut (lock nut), then take up on the ferrule to reduce lever travel to about ¾ inch. Then tighten up on the lock nut. When you do this, make certain there is another 1 inch of "takeup" left under the ferrule. If there isn't, it is best to take up at the brake drum, as will be discussed in the paragraph on "Secondary Adjustment."

The foot brake generally has no adjustment at the brake pedal itself. Take up is made at the drum. Trace the thin rod running from the foot pedal back to the drum. Take up enough on the threaded rod to reduce pedal travel to about ¾ inch.

With all the lock nuts secure, lift the front wheel and spin it to make certain the front brake isn't dragging. Then make a similar check of the rear wheel.

The reason why it is advisable not to take up all the way at the hand lever or at the foot brake itself (if there is an adjustment there) is that some adjustment should be left in the controls, where changes can be more readily made in the field than at the drums themselves.

Secondary Adjustment. When brake control lever and pedal

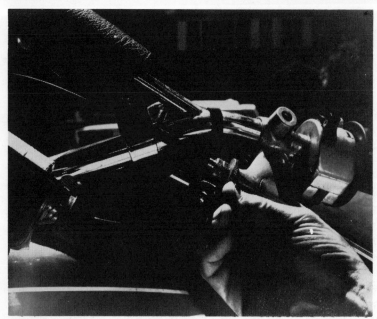

Adjusting the brake cable at the handlebar control lever.

travel can no longer be corrected at the controls (with something to spare), travel is corrected at the drums. You'll find a long bolt at the front drum attached to the end of the control cable. You simply take up on this bolt after you have released the adjustment at the hand lever. In other words, the adjustment at the lever takes up the slack in little bites, the adjustment at the drum takes up the slack in bigger bites.

The same procedure is followed at the rear brake drum.

Precautions. As you take up on the control cable and rod, you will notice that the threaded rods go farther into the arm attached to the brake-shoe cam. When the cam has been turned about 70 degrees, it is time to replace the brake shoes.

There may be some useful brake shoe left, but if the cam is turned any farther it will go past its high point and the brake will not release—it will remain engaged.

If your wheel squeaks and squeals before the cam arm

reaches this point, that is a sign the shoes have worn down to the rivets and should be replaced.

Another indication that it is time to give baby new shoes is the amount of thread left to take up on the control rod or cable. If they are almost through the hole in the cam arm, there is no more "take up" left, so it is wise to change the shoes before you encounter trouble.

Dragging Brakes. Assume that you have taken up a little on the brakes and have given the two wheels the routine test for drag and find that one or both drag. In such a situation the wheel bearings could be at fault or the tire may be rubbing against something. But if all else clears and the wheel(s) still won't turn freely, the fault is probably in the brakes.

If that is the case, disconnect the control cable and/or rod at the brake drum. This leaves the cam arms free. Now spin each wheel in turn. If the brake still drags, try pulling the cam arm in the direction opposite to that required to brake the wheel. If that clears the wheel, if you can't feel the inner springs pull against the cam arm in the normal travel direction, your trouble is inside. If you can feel the springs and merely removing the control rod and cable clears the wheel, the problem lies in the controls.

There are two sets of springs to each mechanical brake. One spring or set of springs normally pulls against the control. This is the spring that lifts the brake pedal and opens the brake grip. If these are broken, if the cable and rod are stuck or jammed, the brake remains engaged once you engage it. Find and clear the jam in the controls. Replace the springs if necessary.

The second set of springs is located inside the brake drums. They pull the brake shoes toward one another and in doing so free the drum. If these springs are weak, broken, or have jammed somehow, the shoes remain pressed against the drums after the brake has been released. You must then dismantle the drum to get to these springs. Once you find them they are easily replaced. When you replace them, be certain that the spring ends point toward the brake plate—the nonrotating part.

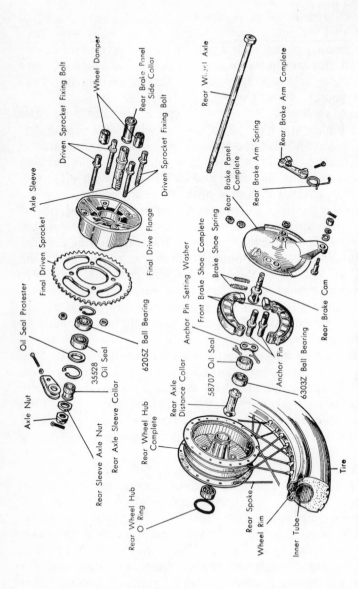

Exploded view of rear wheel assembly of the Honda 250 Scrambler.
Courtesy Honda

Replacing Mechanical Brake Shoes

In order to replace or inspect the shoes or to replace the springs, it is necessary to disassemble the brake drum. Each bike is different, of course, but the general approach is the same.

Disassembling the Front Brake. Remove the control cable and the speedometer cable. Then disconnect the torque arm, remove the cotter pin and the axle nut and then the axle itself. Slide the front wheel out from the fork and with the wheel on its side, cam arm or arms topside, lift the brake plate. Next turn the brake plate over and you will see the brake assembly.

Use care to unhook the springs. Next remove any fasteners used to hold the brake shoes on their pivots. This done, turn the cam arm to separate the shoes and lift them off.

Disassembling the Rear Brake. After removing the master link on the chain and then the chain itself, follow the same procedure as with the front wheel.

Examining the Brake Shoes. If both shoes are not worn to approximately the same degree—though they will show wear in different areas—and you have dual cams, it is likely the two cams are not properly adjusted. We will do that shortly. If the shoes are not worn down to about $\frac{1}{16}$ inch or less at the low spots, it is possible that there is something wrong with the controls. They may be worn or loose so that you work the levers fine but little happens at the brake end. Check this out. All bike brakes will not wear down to the last bit, but most do before the cam reaches a dangerous angle.

At the same time, examine the faces of the cams. If they are worn or rough, or if they are sloppy in their holes, they must be replaced.

As for the worn shoes themselves, they are simply replaced. If, for one reason or another, you aren't going to replace them, you can roughen their surfaces with a coarse file. This makes them function better since filing removes any glaze that may have accumulated.

Reinstalling the Brake Shoes. The brake plate and drum are

Taking up on the front wheel brake cable. Note slot through which you
watch to check on brake lining wear.

wiped or blown clean of dust and brake particles. The two new
shoes or old shoes with new or old linings (the frictive material on the face of the shoes) are replaced in exactly their
original positions. The cam or cams are turned so that the
shoes are spread their minimum distance. Whatever means
were used to hold the shoes on their pivots are replaced. (If
this sounds too general, remember there are hundreds of different mechanical brake designs used on bikes today, and this
is a guide to all bikes and not one specific model.) Next, the
springs are installed, with points facing toward the plate. Now
try the cam arm(s). See that they rotate freely.

If there are two cams and arms, you might check at this
time to make certain both are properly synchronized. Just look

at the cams and see that both are at minimum (the ovals are in their most narrow position between the brake-shoe ends at the same time). If not, adjust the connecting rod accordingly.

When this has been accomplished, the brake assembly is re-positioned within its drum and the drum and wheel are returned to their respective positions within the fork.

Reconnecting the Controls. After the wheels have been re-mounted and the torque bars bolted in place, spin each wheel to "hear" that everything is clear inside. Reconnect the control cable and control rod, providing the maximum slack possible. The procedure that follows is the same for both front and rear brake, so we won't repeat.

Spin the wheel. It should spin silently and free (the chain is still off the rear wheel). Try the brake control. If nothing happens, take up on the brake-drum end of the control mechanism. Spin the wheel and try the control again. Repeat with slight, incremental adjustments until there is ¾ of an inch of free travel in the control before the brake begins to take hold. Then tighten up on the lock nuts. The final step is to spin the wheel and listen carefully for any drag. There shouldn't be any.

DISC BRAKES

Two types of disc brakes are used—mechanical and hy-draulic. The mechanical brake has a disc fastened to the wheel with a "caliper" fastened to the frame astride it. Inside the caliper there is a brake friction pad located on either side of the disc. When you move the hand lever, a cable operates a mechanism inside the caliper that squeezes both brake pads against the disc between them.

The hydraulic brake is somewhat the same. Coupling be-tween the hand lever and brake pads is through a hydraulic circuit. When you squeeze the lever you force a piston into a cylinder, which drives oil through a pipe into a second cylinder or a pair of cylinders inside the calipers. These cylinders press the brake pads against the disc between them. When you re-lease the hand lever, a spring at the master cylinder(the one nearest the control) brings its piston back into place. And at the disc, springs within (usually) each cylinder bring the little pistons back into no-brake position.

Servicing Mechanical Disc Brakes. Essentially the same procedure is used with mechanical discs as with mechanically operated drum brakes. When the control lever swings too close to the handle bars—say two inches or less—before effective brake action starts, you take up at the control lever by adjusting the thumb nuts you find there.

When you have used up most but not all of the "adjustment" on the handlebars, you go to the adjustment at the end of the cable at the calipers. But before you take up cable slack here, use a flashlight, if you can, to get a glimpse of the brake pads. If they are thin, replace them. If not, take up on the cable, after backing off at the handlbars. You want that adjustment handy for quick, in-the-field correction.

To replace the pads on many of the Hondas you simply remove the front wheel and take the calipers apart. Then you remove the cotter pin. The procedure on most of the other bikes is somewhat similar. It is a simple take-apart and replace deal.

After you have replaced the caliper and the wheel, spin the wheel and listen for any contact between the pads and the disc. There should be none when the brake is released. If you get spotty contact—at certain portions of the disc only—chances are the disc is warped (heat from consistent overbraking can do it).

Servicing Hydraulic Disc Brakes. The basic mechanism is similar to that used on a car. The master cylinder must be kept filled with hydraulic brake fluid. Any smell of alcohol near the mechanism indicates a leak, which can be in the line or at any of the cylinders. In any case, a leak spells trouble because the fluid will squirt out and you will not be able to develop pressure at the calipers.

To replace the pads the caliper must be carefully disassembled. A special tool can be purchased for keeping the pads and the pistons behind them in place as you do this, but you can get by with a wedge of wood.

The caliper is removed, and you must keep advancing the wedge as you slip the wheel and disc out. Then the pads are replaced one at a time. If you can keep the fluid from leaking out past the caliper pistons, you simply reassemble. If you have lost some fluid, there is a chance air has gotten into the line, and you will have to bleed it.

To bleed after everything has been reassembled, you press on the brake lever, simultaneously opening the bleed plug on the brake calipers. Watch the stream of fluid squirt out. When it runs solid and bubble free, that signifies all air has been expelled from the lines, so shut it off in mid-flow.

Should your hand lever fail to develop brake pressure, either your master cylinder or the caliper cylinders are defective. Replace.

9

Steering and Suspension

STEERING ASSEMBLY

The front fork is carried by two sets of ball bearings mounted inside the steering stem. The bearings permit the front fork to rotate easily from side to side while preventing it from moving up and down.

To prevent the front fork from rotating too quickly from side to side it is usually "damped." Should you strike a rock a glancing blow with your front wheel, the damping mechanism will prevent the front fork and handlebars from swinging wildly to one side and possibly causing your cycle to flip. On rough roads the damping mechanism prevents or at least reduces the tendency for the handlebars to swing back and forth —shimmy—and shake up you and the bike.

Two types of damping mechanisms are used—friction and hydraulic. In the first type friction is developed between a circular plate integral with the front fork and a second plate bolted or welded to the underside of the steering stem. One plate rubs against the other and slows the side-to-side movements of the fork. Generally there is a large knob atop the center of the steering stem that enables the rider to vary the damping (friction). One simply tightens for more friction and loosens for less.

While this arrangement is simple and light in weight, it presents equal resistance to all turning speeds. A better response is provided by the hydraulic system. This comprises a small piston within a cylinder (shock absorber) fastened to the underside of the front of the frame and the front fork. Turn a hydraulically dampened steering fork slowly from side to side and you encounter no resistance. Try to turn it rapidly and the handlebars fight back. This is, of course, the more desirable response.

Servicing the Steering Assembly. Approximately once each year the front wheel should be taken off and the steering fork removed from the steering stem. The two rings of bearings are then repacked with grease and reassembled. The front fork is replaced and the cap nut is carefully screwed down. You must have enough pressure on this nut to make certain the fork cannot move up and down. There should be no play at this point. At the same time, the rotating joint should not bind.

Adjusting the front wheel friction-damping knob.

This is best accomplished with the front wheel off, the friction adjustment at minimum and, if there is a hydraulic damper, it should be disconnected. Afterwards, be certain to replace and tighten the lock nut.

SPRINGS

The purpose of a spring is to enable your front wheel or rear wheel to move up and down in response to road shocks and changing loads. The purpose of the shock absorbers is to slow the spring's response. You want the spring to move but you don't want it to bounce. In a sense, a spring is like a rubber ball. Drop it on concrete and it bounces. Put a small hole in the ball and drop it onto the ground and it no longer bounces. The combination of spring and damping enables the spring to absorb the shock without rebound. Put another way, without shock absorbers you would be thrown every time your bike hit a bad bump.

Two types of springs are currently used. One type has even spacing between its windings. The other has varied spacing. The first is called regular and its response to compression is fairly regular. The other is called progressive and it gives easily at first, resisting with increasing force as it is compressed. The regular or straight spring is often found on heavy street machines. The progressive spring is more often installed on trail bikes and lighter machines. In some designs a lighter booster spring is added to the regular spring, resulting in spring action that more or less equals that of a progressive spring.

You'll find bikes with external springs bared for all the world to see. You'll find other bikes with external springs hidden beneath boots. Finally, there are bikes with their springs sited within telescoping metal tubes that also enclose or even comprise the shock absorbers.

The visible springs are easier to replace, generally. Also, you can see them sag when they become aged. However, many of the internal springs can be corrected for sag by simply turning a large screw pushing down on their upper ends.

Servicing Springs. Except for taking up whatever sag develops over the years, nothing needs to be done to or with springs. So long as they aren't broken and hold to their original size, they are fine.

SHOCK ABSORBERS

Shock absorbers used on motorcycles are very similar to those found on automobiles. They consist of a piston within a cylinder (tube) filled with oil. The piston will have a number of small holes plus a valve. The cylinder is closed at one end.

When the piston is pushed into the cylinder slowly, the oil flows through the holes and very little resistance is encountered. The amount of resistance varies with the speed of the piston. The faster you try to move it, the harder it is to move. At the end of the stroke the valve enables the oil to return to its original position when the piston goes back to its original position.

Although all shock absorbers work more or less the same way, they are grouped into single- and double-damping types. The difference is based on the shock's resistance to up-and-down wheel movement. If the shock is constructed or adjusted so that it lets the wheel bound upward toward the bike frame but greatly resists the wheel and attached spring's return to normal, the shock is called single action. On these shocks the ratio of upward resistance to downward resistance may be 1 to 9.

On the double-damping designs the ratio of upward to downward resistance to motion will be on the order of about 3 to 7. The single-damped shocks are generally used with progressively wound springs for street and fairly gentle trail riding. The double-damped shocks are generally used with regular springs in bikes that are going to see a lot of rough service.

Adjusting the Shocks. Some shocks have external controls that permit the rider to vary the size of the holes passing the oil. They are more expensive but you can "tune" your bike to road conditions.

Servicing Shocks. Some shocks cannot be adjusted or repaired. They are discarded and replaced when they lose their

An adjustable rear shock absorber.

oil or no longer work properly. Other types have provisions for draining and replacing their oil. This should be done about once a year. Still other shocks can be taken apart and the O-rings, which help seal the oil in place, çan be replaced when worn.

Incidentally, you will know when your shocks stop working—you'll bounce up and down every time you hit a hole or bump.

LEADING-LINK FRONT FORKS

To reduce the bashing a front fork takes when it encounters a bump or pothole, many manufacturers have provided their bikes with leading-link front forks. Very simply, the front axle rides on a pair of levers that swing on the ends of the front fork. Sometimes called Earle's forks, after their inventor, they save the bike and its rider a great deal of jarring, but they do add weight to the bike and require extra care.

Servicing Leading Links. Check the bolts on the linkage to make certain they are tight. Test the linkage for play. You'll have to take the weight off the front wheel to do this. Lubricate the linkage regularly as per owner's manual.

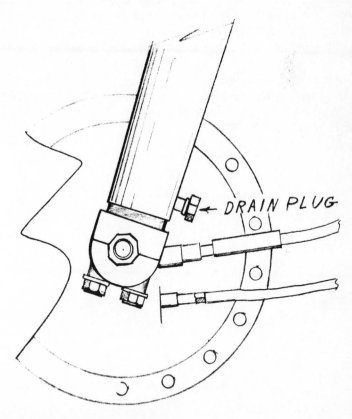

Position of drain plug on front fork.

Rear Fork

Sometimes known as the rear swing arm, the rear fork
carries the rear wheel and associated parts. It swings from a
long transverse bolt that may pass through the frame and may
pass through a hole in the engine itself. The rear fork swings
up and down with changes in bike loading and road variations.

The two shocks and the two springs attached to the rear
fork work just like those up front, though they usually do not
look alike. There are, however, some exceptions. Some rear
shocks are gas-filled. They use gas in place of oil as a damping
medium. (You'll find Hondas and other bikes with these
shocks.) When gas-filled shocks lose their damping ability,
don't fool with them, replace them with oil-filled shocks of the
same size and capacity.

Servicing the Rear Fork. Outside of making certain the bolt
that serves as an axle is tight and properly lubricated, there is
nothing to do.

10

The Fuel System

The fuel system on a modern motorcycle is at once simpler and more effective than the fuel system on a modern automobile. Motorcycle fuel systems have no fuel pumps. Fuel flows by gravity alone from the fuel tank into the carburetor. Automobiles have complicated, fixed-venturi jet carburetors. Motorcycles have simpler carburetors with variable-venturi jets. The variable venturi provides an increase in fuel much more closely related to increasing engine rpm than the fixed venturi. It would appear that variable venturi would also be used on automobiles, but it isn't, for reasons beyond this writer.

TYPES OF CARBURETORS

All the motorcycle engines carry variable-venturi jet carburetors. The difference between the various makes and designs of carburetors lies mainly in how the jet is varied. The better-known designs are described below.

Direct-Control, Slide-Valve Carburetors. This type of carburetor is readily recognized by the position of the control cable, which almost, if not always, enters from the top and is directly connected to the slide valve.

Three slide-valve designs are used, but they all work the same way. Several, like Mikuni, IRZ, Bing, and others, use a hollow metal tube as their slide mechanism. Others, such as Lake and Pos-a-Fuel, use a flat metal plate with a circular hole through its middle. This simple design is sometimes called a guillotine. And still other manufacturers, like Amal, for example, use a solid metal bar or piston with a circular hole cut through its thickness.

When you twist the throttle, you raise the slide valve and move the hole in line with the air passage leading from the air filter to the intake manifold or directly to the cylinder. In the case of the cylinder valve, the cylinder is lifted clear of the air passage. When you release the throttle, the solid portion of the slide valve or the slide itself covers the air passage and very little air gets to the engine—ergo, the engine slows to idle.

If you will recall the automotive carburetor, you will remember that a small pipe with a very fine hole, called the venturi, leads from the fuel bowl into the aforementioned air stream. When air passes over the open end of the venturi, fuel is drawn along into the engine.

The bike's carburetor also has a venturi and it, too, works the same way, but with an important difference. The bike's venturi is variable. The bottom of all the slide valves we just mentioned have long, thin control-jet needles. These fit into the venturis.

When the slide is in the lowered position and the air passage to the engine is almost closed off, the venturi is almost closed by the control needle. As the throttle is turned and the slide is lifted and more air is admitted to the engine, the control needle is lifted and more fuel comes out of the venturi. As the slide valve is lifted still higher, the needle continues upward, releasing still more fuel. Thus the motorcycle engine is fed an increasing amount of fuel as the engine speeds up.

In the auto carb the increase in fuel is solely dependent upon the vacuum generated in the venturi. The auto carb's venturi is fixed. The bike's carb has a variable venturi. This results in smoother power over a wider range of engine speed.

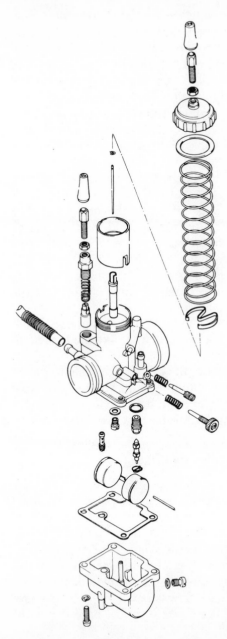

Amal carburetor used by
Suzuki on its GT750. *Courtesy
Suzuki*

CV, or Constant-Vacuum, Carburetors (also called constant-velocity). Outwardly the telltale feature of the CV carb is the control cable-to-lever connection at its side. The lever is attached to a butterfly valve, which is merely a disc pivoted at its center. When the engine is at idle, the disc is in a vertical position almost completely closing the air passage leading from the air filter past the venturi to the cylinder or manifold. When the throttle is twisted, the disc valve is turned to a a horizontal position. The valve offers minimum resistance to air flow and the engine revs to maximum. Note that the throttle cable is attached to the butterfly valve and nothing else.

The jet control needle is attached to the underside of a piston positioned within a cylinder connected by a passage to the engine side of the carburetor's air stream. When the engine is at idle, the piston is in its "down" position. When the throttle is turned, the engine speeds up. As it does, a partial vacuum is produced above the piston. It moves upward and lifts the control needle out of the venturi.

In some designs the piston is replaced by a diaphragm. From the outside these carburetors look somewhat like the tops of an aumotive fuel pump.

The CV carburetor came into the cycling game shortly after 1966. The first CV's were to be found on the Honda 450. Now many bikes have them. CV carbs are manufacture by Keihin, Mikuni, Del Orto, and Bing, just to name a few companies.

Four Systems or Circuits

Each carburetor has what may be defined as four somewhat independent systems or circuits. They are start, low speed, midrange, and high speed.

Start Circuit. To provide the richer than normal fuel/air mixture necessary for starting a cold engine, various methods are used. The simplest is merely a choke, which is a second valve in the main air passage leading the the cylinders.

When this valve is closed, air flow is restricted, thus increasing the ratio of fuel to air. The choke on a CV carb is usually

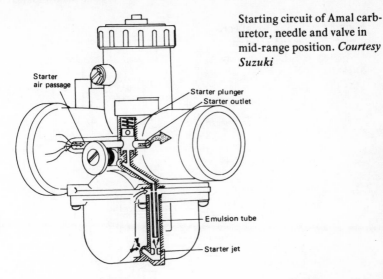

Starting circuit of Amal carburetor, needle and valve in mid-range position. *Courtesy Suzuki*

in the form of a second butterfly valve operated by an individual control. On some direct-control slide-valve carbs the choke is a metal plate that is slid across the incoming air stream.

Unfortunately, all the carbs do not rely on chokes for starting; some have more complicated systems, as the illustrated example of the Amal used on the Suzuki GT750. This carb has a starter plunger, among other components, which is cable-operated.

Low Speed or Idle. At idle the hand throttle is released. The slide valve is in its "down" position and the main jet is more or less sealed off by the control needle. Since the slide valve is never fully closed—some have cut-out portions preventing this—a little air reaches the engine from this source. Additional air is admitted by the idle air inlet controlled by the pilot air screw or the idle air screw. Fuel reaches the engine through the pilot jet or the slow-running jet or the idle jet. (Each carb maker gives his product his own descriptive terms.)

Alternately, on a CV carb, idling may be accomplished by

Main jet system of Amal carburetor, needle and valve in mid-range position. *Courtesy Suzuki*

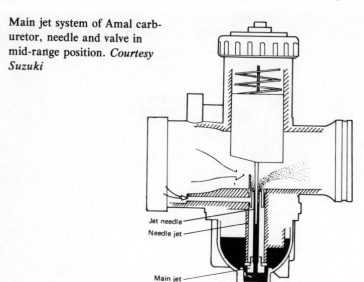

Jet needle
Needle jet
Main jet

an adjustable stop holding the butterfly valve open a fraction—just as it is done on an automobile—and an idle jet.

Mid-Range. You have cracked the throttle a bit and the engine is possibly at its middle rpm speed. The slide valve is partially open and the control needle is partially out of its venturi. The comparatively vast quantity of air and fuel that is now drawn by the engine "swamps" the tiny amount supplied by the idling circuit and in that way the idling system is rendered ineffective or switched out.

High Speed. The slide valve is now completely open and the control needle is all the way out. The engine is receiving as much fuel and air as it can manage and is going full speed.

FLOAT SYSTEM

To prevent the fuel from overrunning the carburetor, an automatic valve is inserted into the line leading from the fuel tank to the fuel bowl on the carburetor. The valve is merely a tiny metal float that swings on a pivot and actuates a tiny needle valve. When the bowl is filled with fuel, the float rises and pushes the needle valve closed against the valve seat, preventing more gasoline from entering the fuel bowl.

MULTIPLE CARBURETORS

Bike designers add carburetors to multi-cylinder engines to provide each cylinder with more fuel mixture and to distribute the fuel to the cylinders more evenly than is possible with a single carburetor. Should the fuel be unevenly distributed, a condition that doesn't readily occur, the engine may vibrate and the overworked cylinder will run hotter than the rest.

The simplest method of checking on dual carburetors is to run the engine until it is warm, have a friend hold it at about 3,000 rpm, and then place one of your palms about 5 or 6 inches from each of the dual exhausts. The pressure produced should be about the same. Just be careful you don't burn yourself.

The other methods include examining the aligning marks provided by the manufacturer on the carburetors. Generally there is a hole through which you look to see a mark on the valve. When all the marks are where they are supposed to be, the carbs are synchronized. The trouble with this method is that you have to know where and how to look, which means you must have the manufacturer's instructions.

SERVICING THE CARBURETOR

Before you even think about servicing the carburetor (proper), be advised that it is probably the most reliable piece of equipment on your bike. Except for the passage of fuel and air and the small swing of the float on its pivot, nothing wears. So if your bike isn't feeling its oats, don't jump on the carburetor.

Be advised that ignition and valve changes and especially changes in the air filter will effect engine operation. Most

noticeable is the slowing down of the engine at idle. So before
you readjust the idling controls, check everything else out first.

The sum of the foregoing is that the first service instruction
regarding carburetors is leave them alone.

The second, and this one is important, is keep the fuel clean.

Normally the gasoline you receive from your local station
is clean, but in these days of make-believe gas shortages, many
of the independent stations run dry. If you are unfortunate
enough to buy the last few gallons, you get the rust, muck, and
water thrown in without charge. The muck clogs the filters and
jets, the abrasive particles enlarge the venturi and shorten the
control needle. The rust and the water combine to produce pin
holes in your gas tank and fuel bowl float.

To prevent all this, clean your fuel filter and fuel bow every
month or two. To drain the fuel bowl, shut off the gas, place
a clean rag beneath the carburetor, and either unscrew the
large brass plug to get at the filter or push the snap fastener
aside—if that is where the bowl is located. On some carbs
the bowl is on the side.

Be careful not to lose or damage any of the gaskets when
you remove the filter and bowl. Blow the screens clean. If that
procedure doesn't work, use a little fresh gasoline. When you
return all the parts to their proper place, open the gas valve
and let enough time go by to make certain no joint is leaking.

Your fuel filter may be in-line, in which case you can usually
see its condition. Or it may be beneath the fuel shut-off valve.
In either case you should disconnect the gas hose at the carb
and drain the fuel tank of gas before disassembling the fuel
filter.

Setting Idling Speed

It is assumed that the bike is in excellent running condition,
that plugs, ignition, and air filter are all functioning properly
when you adjust idling speed. If they are not, idling speed will
be adversely affected. That is to say, idling will be slower than
it should be though the carb is properly adjusted.

And, since there are probably more than a hundred different

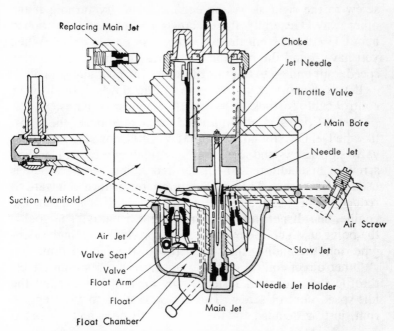

Replacing Main Jet

Choke

Jet Needle

Throttle Valve

Main Bore

Needle Jet

Suction Manifold

Air Screw

Air Jet

Valve Seat

Valve

Float Arm

Slow Jet

Float

Needle Jet Holder

Float Chamber

Main Jet

Details of the carburetor used on the Honda 250 Scrambler. Note slow jet and air screw, both of which are used to adjust idle speed. *Courtesy Honda*

carburetors in use today, the following guidance is general. For specific instructions you will have to refer to your owner's manual.

CV Carb Idling Adjustment. Start the engine and let it warm up. Turn the throttle stop screw (which controls the amount of fuel/air mixture the engine gets) in a direction to bring engine rpm to 1,200. The throttle stop screw is on the lever at the end of the throttle cable. Now turn the pilot screw on the carburetor (which controls the ratio of fuel/air mixture at idling speed) a quarter turn clockwise. (This is the little screw with a spring under it.) Clockwise rotation usually makes the fuel/air mixture more lean at idling speed.

If the engine speeds up, go back to the throttle screw and use it to slow the engine back to 1,200 rpm. If turning the pilot screw to the right slows the engine down, try turning it the other way. Generally these screws are properly positioned about 1½ turns from their bottom (use fingers only). When you have found the position that gives you maximum engine speed, quit and go to the throttle screw for final adjustment.

If you cannot get your engine to idle slowly enough, your control cable is stuck or too short and must be adjusted.

Direct-Control, Carb-Idling Adjustment. Some of the carbs, like the Del Orto found on the BMW R90S, have throttle slide-valve stop screws and idle mixture regulating screws. The slide screw is first adjusted to the desired idling speed, which is usually 1,200 rpm. Then the mixture screw is turned inward to reduce the percentage of fuel drawn at idle. If that speeds the engine, fine. If not, turn the screw the other way. The goal is the point at which the mixture screw produces the highest engine rpm; then adjust the slide screw to the desired rpm.

Other direct-control carbs do not have a screw that affects throttle slide position. Instead, they have a screw called the idle-speed control screw. This screw is used to vary engine rpm, just as detailed for the previous throttle and slide-stop

The projecting screw under the screwdriver adjusts the position of the slide valve at idle. Valve cable enters carb from its top.

screws. They also have a mixture-control screw, which is again "worked" as spelled out for the same screw control on the carburetors previously described.

One difficulty you may encounter with a carb you haven't seen before or for which you have no data is control screw identification. Generally, the screw that projects beyond the carb body controls the position of the slide valve at idle. The screw that is flush usually controls the fuel/air mixture. Also, backing the fuel/air mixture screw outward usually increases the flow of fuel.

Some carbs have idle fuel-mixture adjust screws and idle air-adjustment screws. Be advised that there is no way of telling them apart by merely turning them. Since you are striving for maximum idling speed, it is possible to get top speed with the wrong adjustment (too much air).

When you have too lean a mixture, the engine hesitates or stumbles as you go from idle to mid-range or higher. Also, the engine may backfire inside the carburetor. These effects do not always occur when the mixture is too lean, but if one or both occur, you can be certain of it.

In any event, don't adjust your carb too lean. A lean mixture tends to raise temperature and burn the valves on a 4-stroke engine. On a 2-stroke, in which the lube oil is mixed with the fuel, too lean a fuel/air mixture will let the engine run dry and possible burn itself out.

Mid-Range and Full-Speed Adjustments

In most instances it is necessary to partially or completely disassemble the carburetor to alter the fuel/air mixtures it feeds the engine at mid-range and full speed. On some carbs the height of the needle above the main jet is varied. The greater the distance of the needle out of the jet, the more gasoline is passed. On some carbs it is necessary to change needles to alter the fuel/air mixture, while other carbs require that both the needle and the main jet be changed. However, it is unnecessary and unwise to make these changes to your carburetor unless you have modified the engine.

As discussed previously, the control needle is affixed to the slide valve. Unless something has worked loose, the only change that can occur is one caused by either wear or clogging. Normally, wear is insignificant. The frictive quality of fuel that is, in itself, an oil (and may have added oil) after it has passed at least two filters is negligible. Clogging, however, is another matter. The venturi orifice is small to begin with. Dirt in the fuel and fuel evaporating within the carburetor can reduce the venturi opening.

You can sometimes spot an obstructed venturi by reduced engine power and a tendency of the engine to hesitate when you quickly advance the throttle.

Cleaning the Carburetor. Before you disassemble the carb, make certain there is no obstruction in the fuel line. Dirt in either of the two filters can starve the engine for gas and the result may be indistinguishable from an overly lean fuel/air mixture. At the time you examine the carb's filter, try working the float gently up and down (assuming it is exposed when you get to the filter). There is a chance that a particle of dirt has jammed the float in the partially closed position.

If all this proves useless, there is a chance that the varnish left behind by evaporating fuel has reduced the venturi orifice and the float-valve orifice. Gum and other gasoline deposits can often be removed by a commercial carburetor cleaner. Some types are added to the fuel, others are sprayed into the carburetor intake. None can do any harm; just exercise care to keep the cleaner off the paint job.

Checking Mid-Range and Full-Speed Carb Action—There are two simple methods you can use for roughly determining whether or not your carb is doing its proper thing at mid-range and top engine rpm. Both procedures assume that all is well and only the carburetor is suspected of malfunctioning.

The first requires your adjusting the engine idle screw to bring the engine up to about half speed, or hold the throttle steadily at half speed. Then slowly close the choke. If the engine accelerates, the fuel/air mixture is probably too lean.

The other method simply involves examining your spark plugs. If everything appears okay and the plugs show a lot of carbon, you may be running too rich. If they show a lot of white powder, indicating too much heat, the bike is running too lean.

Both methods presume everything else is operating perfectly, and neither method is by any means exact, but they are useful guides.

Air Filter

The purpose of the air filter is to keep dust and other abrasive particles out of the engine. Unfortunately, the filter robs the engine of power. If you remove the filter completely, you can raise engine power by some 10 percent (assuming the filter is clean and in good condition; much more if it is dirt-sodden).

However, the flow of dust through your engine will shortly ruin it. And the interval to ruination will depend on the amount of dust found on the road you regularly travel. In a really bad situation, you can wear out an engine in a couple of days.

Servicing the Air Filter. Most of the filters are of the dry type. They cannot and should not be washed. All you can do with them, except replace them, is to blow them out gently and shake them lightly to eliminate the dust. Some are sealed inside their holders with a layer of grease. Others carry protective screens. All you need remember with these gadgets is that you must be careful not to damage the filter or get it mucked up. If the pores in the filter are clogged with grease, the filter will not pass air or will pass less air and the engine will not perform properly.

One Way to Increase Engine Power. You can increase your engine's output without rebuilding by installing an air filter with a larger cross section. This allows the engine to "breathe" better and it will put out a little more horsepower.

In addition, you can also install an air ram or scoop (also called velocity tube or horn) which is just what the description implies. It is a scoop facing forward and attached to the air filter. As the cycle whips forward, air is driven into the carburetor in a sort of poor man's supercharger effect. The air scoop should preferably be positioned ahead of the cylinders so that it receives cool air. Cool air is heavier than hot air, and you get more power because there is more of it inside the cylinders.

When you make either or both these changes, your engine will be running leaner, so you will have to alter the mid- and high-range fuel circuits to give the engine more fuel in addition to altering the idling jet.

FUEL TANKS AND VALVES

Fuel flow from the tank to the carburetor is by gravity. Since the flow is through a small-diameter pipe, it is absolutely

Grease on edges of this washable-type filter helps seal out air.

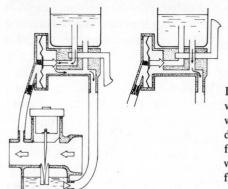

Inside a vacuum-controlled fuel valve. Drawing on left shows valve in run position with diaphragm controlling flow of fuel. Drawing on right shows valve in start position; fuel flows directly down to carburetor. *Courtesy Suzuki*

necessary that the fuel tank be open to the air. If it isn't, a vacuum will form and no gasoline will flow into the carburetor. Therefore, all cycle gas caps have small holes. If the hole is plugged or if you have somehow attached the wrong cap, you will find that the bike will start and run normally for a short distance before stopping. Then, after you unscrew the gas cap and check for gas, the engine will start again and run once again for a short distance. The cure is to unplug the hole or install a cycle gas cap.

Ground-Key Valves. If your petcock reads simply *on* and *off,* you have a ground-key fuel valve, which is a smooth metal plug with a hole in it. These valves rarely leak. When they do, it is usually because the plug is loose. Tightening the nut found on the other side of the plug sometimes helps.

Automatic Fuel Valves. These read *off, prime,* and *run.* In the off position no gasoline flows. In the prime position the fuel line is open to the carburetor. In the run position the flow of fuel is controlled by engine speed. The prime position is used when the cycle has stood about several hours and there may be little or no gasoline in the carb's fuel bowl. The run position is used when the engine is still warm from the previous ride and, of course, once the engine has been started and is operating.

Engine speed is made to control fuel flow by means of a vacuum and needle valve system. A pipe from the engine side of the carburetor is connected to a closed chamber, one side of which is a diaphragm. A needle valve is connected to the other side of the center of the diaphragm. As the engine accelerates, the vacuum developed moves the diaphragm and its needle valve away from the valve seat. Thus the carb gets more fuel at high engine rpm than at low and thus the control of fuel into the carb's fuel bowl is not limited to the float.

The trouble with the float is that while it does rise and fall with fuel level, it also moves up and down with bumps in the road. That is why it is possible to have a flooded carburetor even though the float is working properly.

TROUBLESHOOTING THE FUEL SYSTEM

No Fuel in Carburetor
> Gas cap hole plugged.
> Fuel valve incorrectly adjusted (handle on wrong).
> Vacuum pipe to valve off, leaking air, or plugged.
> Fuel filter(s) plugged.
> Fuel float incorrectly adjusted or stuck in closed position.
> Fuel needle valve stuck in closed position.

Insufficient Fuel in Carburetor
> Gas cap hole partially plugged.
> Vacuum pipe leaking air.
> Fuel filter(s) partially plugged.
> Fuel float incorrectly adjusted.
> Fuel needle valve partially plugged with dirt.

Engine Idles Too Slowly
> Air filter partially clogged.
> Carburetor-to-engine joint leaking air.
> Choke partially closed.
> Idle jet partially clogged.

Engine Idles Too Rapidly
> Air filter ripped.
> Air filter-to-carburetor joint leaking air.

Choke partially closed.

Throttle partially open (no free play).

Engine Hesitates or Stumbles at Start of Acceleration

Idle mixture too lean.

Control needle loose in socket.

High-speed jet loose.

Idle speed too low.

Engine Lacks Power at High RPM

High-speed jet partially clogged.

Control needle loose in socket.

Air filter clogged.

Fuel filter(s) clogged.

Carburetor-to-engine joint leaking air.

Fuel float improperly adjusted.

Wrong control needle.

Wrong high-speed jet.

Control needle improperly positioned.

Reed valve partially jammed.

11

The Engine

Once you have driven your bike beyond its break-in mileage point, its power and efficiency will begin to deteriorate. After a number of miles, their count depending on how you ride and how well you care for your machine, the loss will become first noticeable and then objectionable.

A portion of the loss will have been caused by detrimental changes in ignition, carburetion, and exhaust. The balance of the loss will have occurred in the engine itself—the combination of piston, cylinder, and valves that is the engine proper. The quickest, most accurate way to test the engine itself is to measure its compression and compare it with its specified value.

COMPRESSION TESTING

To measure a cylinder's compression the engine is thoroughly warmed up and then shut off. All the spark plugs are removed. A compression tester is jammed into each spark plug hole in sequence. The engine is then jump-started half a dozen times for each cylinder with the throttle wide open. The first few starts on each cylinder are ignored. Pressure readings for the balance of the starts are averaged.

Compression readings vary from engine to engine and with compression ratios. Engines with higher ratios exhibit higher compression figures. Typically, the 4-stroke Honda 250, with a compression ratio of 9:1, develops 149 psi. The BSA A50 Star, with a compression ratio of 8.5:1, develops 138 psi, while its sister bike, the A65 Star, with a ratio of 7.5:1, develops only 123 psi on a compression test.

Effect of Low Compression

When an engine's compression is low, it will fail to deliver its rated horsepower, it will lack normal acceleration, will consume fuel like crazy, and its exhaust will be heavier and more odorous than normal. If it is a 4-cycle engine, it will burn (use) more lube oil than is customary.

The lower the compression, the worse will be the various

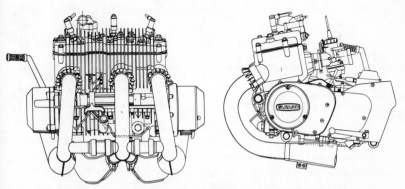

Front and side views of the Suzuki GT750, water-cooled, 2-cycle, three-cylinder engine with an aluminum block and cast-in-place-cylinder liners. *Courtesy Suzuki*

conditions in the foregoing paragraph. And when low compression is the fault, nothing can be done to overcome the condition except to return compression to normal.

Causes of Low Compression

As the piston moves up and down in its cylinder and the valves open and close, they wear. And as they wear the fit between the parts becomes looser and pressure developed by the piston moving upward against the top of the cylinder is reduced.

While wear and the loss of compression, and with it engine efficiency, can be retarded by proper engine operation and lubrication, it cannot be stopped entirely. Senility in the form of lessened power comes to all engines as it does to all humans. Other causes of low compression include burnt valves, improperly adjusted valves, sticking valves, broken piston rings, and piston rings jammed in their grooves.

Determining Cause(s) of Low Compression

First, make certain your pressure gauge is reasonably accurate. It may be reading on the low side. Second, be sure you have the proper figure. Don't estimate or guess your engine's compression rating. Third, take sufficient readings to enable you to get the correct average. And fourth—most important—don't let a 10, 15, or even 20 percent below specifications figure disturb you unless you are dissatisfied with your bike's performance and everything else in the engine checks out fine.

If you have come this far and still want to go farther, back off the adjusting screws on the rocker arms to make certain the valves are fully closed (on a 4-cycle engine). Then test again. Dissassemble the head or whatever is necessary to get a good look at the valves and valve seats. If they are smooth and clean, your trouble is in the cylinder.

If you have a 2-cycle and its compression is low, the trouble lies in the cylinder.

CURABLE CYLINDER TROUBLES

If you have been using too much oil or the wrong oil, there is a slim chance that the rings have become stuck in their grooves. This doesn't happen very often, but when it does the cylinder loses compression because the rings do not make proper contact with the cylinder walls and the gases slip by.

Whether or not your rings are jammed, the cure for stuck rings is simple enough. Run the engine until it is hot. Then remove the plugs and pour into each cylinder either half a glass of pure turpentine or any of the commercial solvents formulated to loosen rings and valves. The following day drain the crankcase, lube up, and try the engine again. Sometimes it works.

If your valves have been adjusted so that they aren't closing, loosening the set screws so they do close will restore compression. (The valves are properly adjusted afterwards.) This condition is rare because valves adjusted so they don't close usually burn out quickly.

If you find the valves (exhaust) are burned out—meaning they have rough edges and do not seat properly so that they do not seal—there is the possibility the valves alone are at fault and the rings are okay. There is also the possibility that both the valves and rings are shot. (We are, of course, speaking of valves on a 4-cycle job.) There is no easy way to determine whether the trouble is both valves and rings or valves alone. However, if the engine is old and the condition developed slowly, it is probably both. If the engine is new, the valves were probably improperly adjusted and therefore burned out.

CHEMICAL COMPRESSION IMPROVERS

There are one or two compounds on the market that are

guaranteed to plate your cylinder's wall with metal of some kind and thus increase or, rather, regain your engine's lost compression. Don't waste your time and money. None of them work. I have tried them and they turn out to be some kind of asphalt or gum that works for only a short interval.

DOING A RING AND VALVE JOB

Although we say the rings are shot or worn when the piston and cylinder has lost compression, the rings alone are never shot. The entire motor is worn. The rings rub on the cylinder walls; therefore, it, too, wears. The piston rides on the connecting rod, which rides on the crankshaft, which rides on its bearings. Ergo, everything is worn. So when compression is gone in an engine (exclusive of stuck rings and burned or maladjusted valves), chances are that the entire engine needs to be overhauled.

If you read the parts catalogs and some of the instruction manuals, the work involved appears simple. You purchase a complete kit of rings and new bearings. You remove the old parts and replace with new, just like an Erector set.

But it isn't that easy. In many instances, you have to rebore the cylinder because it has been worn into an oval. In other instances you must also rebore the connecting rod and regrind the crankshaft. These parts, too, are no longer within tolerance and are no longer perfectly round. The pistons have to be resized.

Every moving joint must be measured and fitted within a specified few thousandths of an inch. Every mating surface must be smooth. If you try to do these things with hand-held tools, if you are not experienced in reading a micrometer, if all you do is get the replacement parts to fit—and this isn't difficult—you will have an engine that will run a few hundred miles and conk out. It is a waste of time and money.

If a valve has broken without damaging the rest of the engine, if a ring has broken and you stop the engine before it has done any damage, if all you have to do is take the engine apart and reassemble it, go to it. If you use great care and keep everything perfectly clean, you should have no trouble. On the other hand, if you are dealing with worn parts—even if it is only a single exhaust valve seat—bring the engine to a qualified automotive machine shop. Don't try to do it yourself.

To save money you might take the engine down for them, after you have made arrangements to do so. However, not all the shops want the bike owner to bring in a sack full of engine parts. It frightens them.

Adjusting 4-cycle Valves

Motorcycle engine valves are very similar to auto engine valves. They are pushed up by a camshaft and pulled closed by a spring. Adjustment is made by altering a set screw (usually) at the end of the rocker arm. The adjustment is always a few hundredths of an inch, so that the end of the push rod or valve stem separates a distance from the end of the rocker arm adjusting screw.

In some engines the adjusting screws and lock nuts are easily reached after removing a cover. In others, you have to reach down and around. But no matter where the adjustments are positioned, or how they have to be made, or how many cylinders there may be, you always use a flat metal feeler gauge to measure the space between valve stem and push rod.

The thickness of the gauge is specified in your owner's manual. You will be given the clearance for the intake and the exhaust valve. Sometimes it will be the same dimension. You will also be informed if the measurement or adjustment is to be made hot or cold. If hot, let the engine warm up for at least fifteen minutes. If cold, let it stand around until the engine feels cool to your touch.

Adjustment, Hot. With the engine idling, you attempt to slip the specified thickness gauge between the tappet end and the rocker arm. If it slips between, you know the space is at least equal to that specified. But don't stop now. Try the next thicker gauge. That shouldn't fit. If it does, you have too much clearance and you need to adjust.

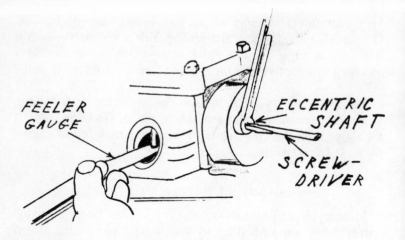

How an eccentric shaft is used to adjust the tappets on the Honda CB500 engine.

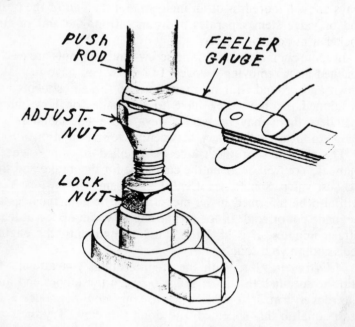

Adjusting the tappets on a Harley-Davidson Sportster.

Loosen the lock nut and turn the screw a fraction, then retighten the lock nut and test again. If the correct gauge doesn't fit, back off a fraction on the screw and test again.

Adjustment, Cold. The same procedure and technique are used here, the difference being that the engine is slowly turned over by hand in its normal direction of rotation.

Hard-to-Reach Adjustments. On some cycle engines the usual 2- to 3-inch gauges are too short to reach between the rocker arm and valve end. On these engines you need the really long gaugues. And on some you will have to bend the feeler gauge to use it. When you do bend the gauge, try to bend it away from the feeler end. You want the end area flat and clean. If it is bent, its effective size has been increased.

On all valve adjustments, remember that if you err a little and overspace the gap between tappet and rocker arm, the valves will be noisy. On the other hand, if you err by making the gap too small, you will burn out your exhaust valves. Better to have noise than burning.

The only valve that requires servicing on a 2-cycle engine is the intake reed valve, if there is one. This is carefully removed and cleaned with either the same solvent used for cleaning plugs or carburetors or carefully scraped clean with a dull knife. And be careful not to bend the reeds.

Removing Carbon

If you are running a 2-cycle job, you will probably want to decarbon the upper cylinder every three months or 6,000 miles. The oil that is added to the fuel carbonizes and collects on the top of the piston and the upper area of the cylinder. It increases compression because it reduces the cylinder's volume. But it also increases internal engine temperature because carbon is an insulator. And it can cause pre-ignition since tiny particles of carbon, once brought to ignition temperature, tend to remain hot. On the plug, of course, it squelches the spark and induces missing.

The 6,000-mile figure is not absolute. You might want to

decarb sooner or later. With experience you will learn what is best for your engine. But you can judge, to some extent, when it first should be done by examining the spark plug, flashing a light into the hole, and gently rubbing a screwdriver across the top of the piston.

With the engine comfortable or cold to the touch, the spark plug and the head bolts are removed. If necessary, the gas tank may be removed, after draining the gasoline. The head may or may not come off easily. In the latter case, try tapping it gently with a screwdriver handle. If that isn't successful, replace the plug and turn the engine over once or twice. Compression may push it up and off. If that still doesn't do it, try working a knife blade between the head and the top of the cylinder, then pry very gently.

Once the head has been removed, use a butter knife to scrape the carbon from its inner side. Then use the edge of the same knife to scrape the carbon from the top of the cylinder. As you scrape, blow the carbon dust to one side. Never use steel wool, sandpaper, or crocus cloth to remove the carbon. These are abrasives and will damage the engine should particles from them get into the crankcase.

Use the same dull knife to remove the old gasket. If it doesn't come off easily, try a little paint remover to loosen it. Just be careful not to drip paint remover on the bike frame. It will penetrate right through the finish and ruin it.

Once the parts are clean, replace the old gasket with a new one, using gasket shellac. Replace the head and take up on the head bolts or nuts. This portion of the work is fairly critical. You should follow the nut-tightening sequence recommended by the engine manufacturer. The sequence is planned to prevent any folds (they will be small but can be troublesome) from developing in the gasket.

If you don't have the proper sequence, work your way outward from the central bolt in a spiral. Or start at one end and lightly tighten all the bolts as you go across. Think of how you would flatten a curled piece of paper.

It is best to follow the manufacturer's instructions on torque. But if you don't have the foot-pound figure, use your own judgment, always remembering that a little less is much safer. After a week of bike riding you can take up some more, but never as tight as you can make them, because you can easily strip the head bolts on a bike engine.

Exhaust Maintenance

From time to time you will need to remove the inner tube in your exhaust(s), clean it, and replace it. The procedure varies from one exhaust design to another, but the basic approach is always the same. The inner rear section is removed, scrubbed clean in gasoline or burned clean over a small fire, and then replaced.

With time the entire muffler will need replacement. There is nothing you can do to prevent this. The alternate heating and cooling, followed by the entrance of moisture in the form of condensation and rain, rusts the iron. It's just a matter of time.

The exhaust pipe is coupled to the engine by means of a finned nut. If it gives you a fight, try a generous dollop of liquid wrench while the nut is cold. If that doesn't work, try heating the nut with a torch while the engine is cold.

Choice of Exhausts. If you use an exact replacement muffler, you should have no problem. If you are running a 2-stroker and switch, you may encounter difficulties. Good mufflers are "tuned" to their engines. They are so calculated that they set up a backward pressure wave timed to meet the incoming fuel charge head on and prevent it from leaving the cylinder and flowing out the exhaust.

If the new exhaust is not timed to your 2-stroke engine, it may reduce your hp although it presents less back pressure to your exhaust flow. Accordingly, to improve your engine's performance your replacement 2-stroke muffler must not only offer less resistance but must also be tuned to your particular engine.

When installing the muffler, take note either to bolt it firmly to the engine or attach it loosely by means of a collar, just as it came off. Some mufflers are fitted tightly against the engine

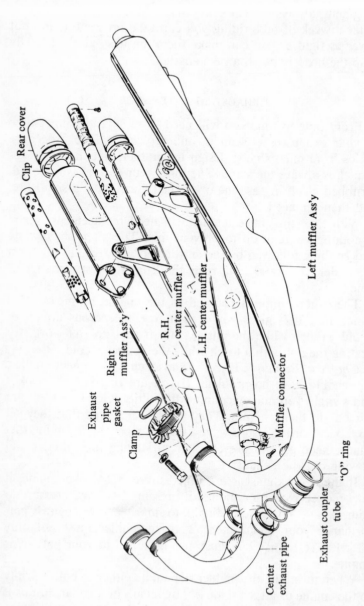

Exhaust system on the Suzuki GT750. *Courtesy Suzuki*

Clip   Rear cover

Exhaust
pipe
gasket

Clamp

Right
muffler Ass'y

R.H.
center muffler

L.H. center muffler

Muffler connector

Left muffler Ass'y

"O" ring

Exhaust coupler
tube

Center
exhaust pipe

block, others are not. Do not interchange because you can crack your block.

4-CYCLE LUBRICATION

The 4-cycle bike engine is lubricated similarly to a conventional automobile engine. The oil is stored in a sump—the crankcase—from which point it is distributed under pressure developed by an oil pump, usually positioned within the crankcase. A portion or all of the circulating oil (it depends on engine design) passes through a replaceable filter outside the engine.

The pump is usually a simple pair of gears and quite efficient and reliable. Most auto engines complete their life cycle from purchase to junkyard without the oil circulating system ever being touched, except for renewing the filter.

Four-cycle motorcycle engines generally perform the same way. All the bike owner need do is change the lube oil at frequent intervals, replace the oil filter, and make certain the crankcase vent is open. The oil is changed while the engine is hot, and 4-cycle engine lube oil is used. In a pinch, a hygrade automotive oil may be used.

2-CYCLE LUBRICATION

Originally the 2-cycle engine was lubricated by adding lube oil to the fuel, generally at a ratio of 1 part oil to 15 parts gasoline. If you didn't add enough oil, your engine ran dry and its wear was accelerated. If you added too much oil, your engine smoked and filled itself up with carbon quite rapidly.

Approximately one hundred years after the 2-cycle engine was invented, a new method of lubing the 2-stroker was introduced. This comprises a small automatic pump that squirts a shot of lube oil into the engine as it runs. The quantity is preset, and so long as you keep the oil tank filled, you have nothing to do.

More recently an improved method of oiling the 2-stroker has made the scene. Instead of squirting oil into the fuel, oil

Removing one feed line of a point lubrication system. Arrow points to a second air-feed connection. Oil must be added to fuel during tests to insure engine lubrication.

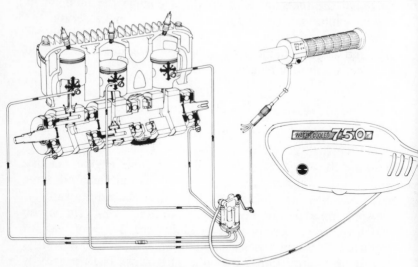

Schematic of the point lubrication system used by Suzuki on their GT750. They call it C.C.I. (Cylinder and Crankshaft Injection). A pump controlled by throttle position drives lube oil under pressure to the six points shown. Preceding photo shows one of them being disconnected for inspection and testing. *Courtesy Suzuki*

is pump-forced into all the engine lube points directly. Each cylinder wall gets a shot, while each bearing on the crankshaft gets its quota. By eliminating the oil in the fuel, the 2-stroke engine has been cleaned up. It doesn't emit as smoky an exhaust and it doesn't carb up as quickly. In fact, it is just about as carbon-free as the 4-stroke.

Judging the Oil Quantity. With the original method you could measure the amount of oil added to the fuel and so be certain your engine was lubricated. With the pump methods you can judge the quantity of lube oil your engine is getting by either carefully watching the rate of oil consumption versus fuel consumption or disconnecting the lube pump's output line and measuring exactly how much oil it squirts.

When you do this, it is advisable to add lube oil to your fuel—say one pint of oil to each gallon of gas—just to be certain your engine is lubed while making the test. The better owner's manuals will give you the exact number of ccs of oil per minute of engine operation at a fixed rpm the lube pump should deliver.

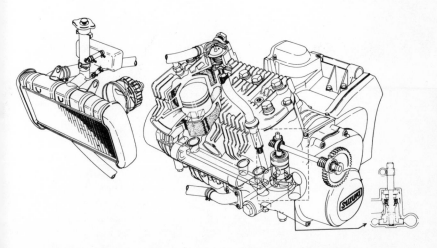

Major portions of the cooling system used on the Suzuki GT750 engine.
Courtesy Suzuki

ENGINE TEMPERATURE

The air-cooled 2- and 4-cycle engines depend on the passage of air over the cylinder and head fins. These fins must be kept clean, and nothing should be tied onto the cycle that interferes with the passage of air through the fins. You don't have to wash them down every other day, but you shouldn't let oil and dirt accumulate on them. Both are insulators and will increase engine temperature.

The water-cooled jobs carry radiators, and this makes them easily recognizable. These engines have the same problems associated with standard auto engines. You must keep the water up to the mark and add anti-freeze in the winter. It is important to watch the thermostat to make certain it is opening properly. If the engine is very hot and the radiator remains cool, you can be certain the stat is closed. Replace.

And, of course, you must keep the radiator clean. Bugs and debris tend to collect in the radiator core, reducing its cooling properties. Push them out gently with a soft piece of wood.

12

The Power Train

The power train is the means whereby the engine's power is transmitted to the rear wheel. In a bike it usually begins at the clutch, which is coupled to the gears by a gear or, more often, by a short loop of chain called the primary chain. From the gears power moves to the rear wheel via a chain sometimes correctly described as the final drive chain, but more often as, simply, the chain.

The BMW does not have a final drive chain. Instead, it has a drive shaft with a bevel gear at each end. The advantage of the drive shaft is that it is fully enclosed and requires very little maintenance. Its disadvantage is that it is mechanically inefficient. It has several times the friction loss of a chain.

Clutch

Most bikes use wet, multi-plate clutches. The basic design consists of a splined shaft attached to or made part of the end of the crankshaft. The splined shaft carries a handful of circular metal plates having serrated holes in their center that fit the splines. When the crankshaft turns, these plates have no option except to turn with it.

A second set of circular plates, having large smooth round holes in their centers and slotted edges, is positioned between each of the first set of plates. A large-diameter, short-length metal tube having a slotted inner surface is sited over all the plates. This tube is attached to a chain or a gear that is, in turn, attached to the gearbox.

Thus we have a set of plates tied by serrations or splines to a shaft fastened to the crankshaft. Interleaved is a second set of plates, free of the crankshaft, but attached to an encompassing tube by circumferential slots. The tube itself is coupled to the gearbox.

As you can visualize, so long as the two sets of interleaving plates do not touch one another, or touch lightly, the engine is free of the gearbox. One set of plates rotates with the engine. The second set just lies there, ignoring everything.

To connect the engine to the gearbox a spring system is used that presses the two sets of plates together. Since they both ride on splines, they easily move together and, since there are a number of plates, the pressure on each doesn't have to be very great because all the pressures and resultant friction are additive.

To provide smooth action and long life the sets of plates are operated within a bath of oil.

On an actual bike a spring or springs will be positioned to normally compress the plates together. Working the clutch lever removes the spring's pressure and permits the plates to rotate free of one another.

Maintenance and Service. All you need do to keep the old clutch functioning properly is to make certain it has the proper share of oil and that the oil is changed at the intervals specified in your owner's manual.

For the clutch to exert all its required pressure when you release the clutch hand lever, there must be at least one-half inch of play in the lever. If not, you can make the necessary correction at the hand lever.

If the clutch slips—that is to say, you can hear the engine accelerate while the bike goes on at more or less its own speed —check to see if there is an adjustment on the clutch itself.

SUZUKI GT750 GEARING DIAGRAM

SPARK PLUG
NGK B-7ES
NIPPON DENSO W22ES

GEAR OIL 2.2ℓ
(4.7 / 3.9 pt. US/ Imp)

IGNITION TIMING 24°$^{+3}_{-2}$
(B.T.D.C.)

TIMING GAUGE STROKE
RIGHT & LEFT 3.64mm
(0.143 in)

MIDDLE 3.42mm
(0.135 in)

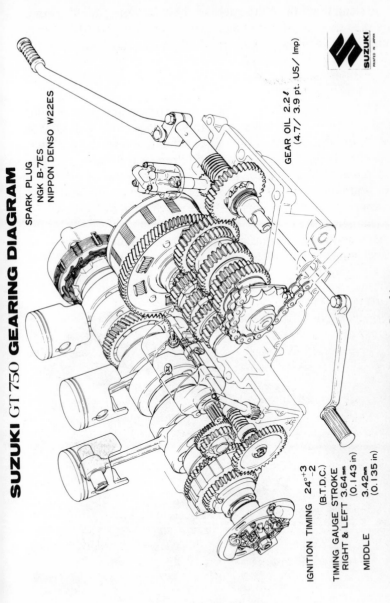

$\mathcal{S}$ SUZUKI
PRINTED IN JAPAN

Gearing schematic of the Suzuki GT750. *Courtesy Suzuki*

If you can't find the adjustment or there isn't one, don't operate the bike as it is. The slippage heats the plates and will shortly ruin them. Bring your pair of wheels to a good bike shop.

GEARS

The gears vary the ratio of engine rpm to rear wheel rpm. You probably remember why this is necessary and how it works from high school physics or you have read the explanation elsewhere, so there is no need to repeat it here.

Changing Gear Ratios. The ratios in your gearbox are fixed, but you can change the ratio between your engine and your rear wheel two ways. You can alter the diameter of your wheel by changing tires and/or rims. If you increase the wheel diameter, you are decreasing the ratio of engine rpm to road travel so that for a given engine speed you will go faster (but

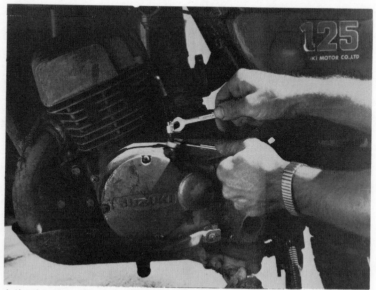

Adjusting the cable controlling the clutch on a Suzuki 125.

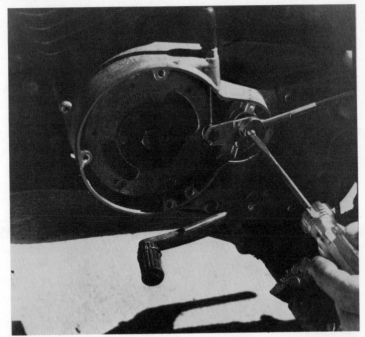

Adjusting the "stroke" on a Suzuki 125 clutch. This makes certain that the movement of the hand control lets the clutch release and engage fully.

have less torque—pulling power). If you reduce the overall wheel diameter, you will go slower for a given engine speed but the bike will perform much better on hills and you'll enjoy better acceleration.

You can also alter the ratio between the engine and the rear wheel by changing the sprocket on the rear wheel. Increasing it by a notch or two slows you down and improves your hill-climbing ability. Reducing sprocket size speeds you up.

Maintenance and Service. There is nothing much to do about gears except to make sure they are taking their oil bath. Use the recommended grade of oil, check its level frequently, and drain while hot so that most of the old oil comes out.

Final Drive Chain

Next to the rider, it's the final drive chain that takes most of the strain of motorcycling. The wear and tear on the chain is so constant and great that some of the bike makers—Kawasaki, for example—suggest the chain be lubricated one or more times every riding day. Whether or not this is necessary probably depends on how much ground you cover each day and the nature of the terrain. But it is a fact that a dry chain can waste as much as 25 percent of your fuel and will wear out very quickly.

Chain Maintenance. Wipe your chain clean every time you run through dust and dirt. If there are chunks of mud, try to get them off without forcing any grime into the chain. And don't forget the rear sprocket. It, too, should be kept clean and lubricated.

Use chain lubricant. It does the best job. In a pinch, use any grease you can obtain—but don't run dry.

Kawasaki also recommends that the chain be removed every 300 to 400 miles, washed clean in a solvent—gasoline for example—and then dried. After that it should be soaked in hot oil to which a little petroleum jelly has been added. Alternately, the chain should be soaked overnight in light engine oil, wiped dry, and then coated with chain lubricant.

Replacing the Chain

The chain should be replaced when it is worn. There are several ways you can determine if it is worn. If you move it sideways, it will bend. A new chain can hardly be moved sideways. If you tighten it, and it becomes loose again in a few days, that signifies excessive wear. If it has loose and stiff spots or sections, it is worn. If you can lift the chain ¼ inch away from the rear sprocket, it is worn. If you put the chain on a new sprocket and it appears to have too many links, or the chain doesn't fit the proper size sprocket, it is worn. If any of the links are cracked, it is ready to break.

If you can pull the chain away from the rear sprocket by ¼ inch, the chain is worn and should be replaced.

When you adjust the tension on the chain, make certain the wheel is centered. Some riders count the number of turns they make with each screw.

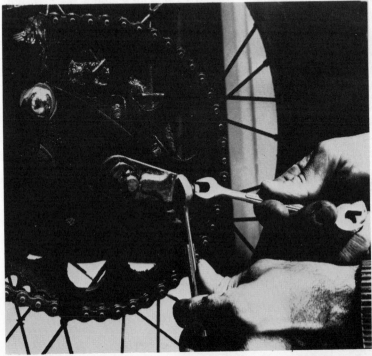

Opening the Chain. Loosen the two axle nuts and the lock nuts on the long set screws that position the axle, then back these screws off an inch or so. This loosens the chain. Now work your way down the length of the chain until you find the connecting link. It looks different from the others. Use a screwdriver and push it forward. This will release two pins. Slip these out and the chain comes apart.

To replace the chain, reverse the process, taking care to keep the opening in the connecting link pointing backward. Next, slowly turn the long set screws an equal number of turns until there is between one-half and one inch of sag in the chain at the mid-point. Following that, make certain that the rear wheel is parallel to the front wheel.

On some bikes the rear wheel will be in the center of the fork. On others it will be offset a little, making space for the rear sprocket. On still others there will be marks on the frame to guide you. No matter how you do it, the rear wheel must be in line with the front wheel. If it is out of line, the bike will not handle properly and your tires will wear out quickly.

Once the rear wheel is positioned, with some slack still remaining in the chain, you lock up shop; tighten the lock nuts and the axle nuts to specified torque.

13

Tune-Up

The purpose of tuning one's engine is to adjust the various components to bring the engine to peak performance. Ostensibly this is a worthwhile endeavor. Why enter a competition with your bike at less that its possible best? Why ride a bike that is wasteful of fuel and doesn't respond as sharply as it could? Ostensibly, tuning doesn't require very much work, so why not do it?

Ostensibly, yes, factually, not always. There are any number of pitfalls on the road to a perfectly tuned machine. To understand and appreciate these pitfalls, let us briefly review the work and problems involved in bringing a machine to its top form.

THE 100% MACHINE

Let us assume that you start with a new engine, run it carefully through its recommended break-in period, and that at the end of that time the machine is at its peak. If you continue to ride the bike after this period, there is nowhere for the engine to go but down. As you continue to ride, you will leave

engine efficiency and peak power farther and farther behind
you. If you take the trouble to measure hp drop, you might
set up a string of descending numbers that could read 95 percent of peak, 90 percent of peak, 85 percent of peak, and so
on down.

With these numbers in mind it is only natural that you will
want to "tune" the engine so as to recover the lost zip. But
can you?

Nonrecoverable HP

Let us say that engine hp is down 10 percent. (This is a
very difficult quantity to measure without a dynomometer but
we need numbers for our discussion.) What portion of this loss
is recoverable and what is not?

Some of the loss is due to piston, cylinder, and valve wear.
You cannot recover losses due to worn pistons, valves, and
cylinders without overhauling these parts. Since engine over-
haul is not a part of engine tune-up, we can call the power lost
because of this wear, nonrecoverable hp.

Recoverable HP

Some of the power loss is caused by a worn or improperly
gapped plug. Some loss is due to air restriction, some due to
exhaust restriction. We can replace the plug, clean or replace
the air filter, and clean the exhaust easily enough. Obviously,
this portion of the missing hp can be recovered.

Some hp loss will be the result of worn and now improperly
adjusted contact breaker points. Some hp erosion will be due
to improper ignition timing, and some loss on a 4-cycle will
be induced by improper valve timing. The latter loss is usually
very small.

All the above losses can be regained if you have the proper
equipment and if you are sufficiently skilled, or if the bike is
far enough out of tune to make inaccuracy unimportant.

Let me explain. Assume your bike is down 10 percent. We
can guess and estimate 2 percent of the loss due to engine wear,

2 percent due to breathing constriction, 2 percent due respectively to maladjusted points and timing, and a final 2 percent the result of worn plug(s).

We cannot recover the engine loss. But we can easily recover breathing by cleaning the air filter and exhaust. The plug presents little problem. That leaves 2 percent lost in the points and timing, etc.

Can you regap the contact breaker points and reset timing so that they are 2 percent closer to the required exact setting? Assuming that we erred in the percentage lost in this portion of the engine, can you reset the timing, etc. 5 percent closer to perfection?

This may have been a long way of making a point, but it may save you lots of time, sweat, and unhappiness. If you haven't the experience or skill to bring the various points of adjustment closer to the correct setting, *leave them alone*.

You cannot detect a 3 or even 5 percent improvement in engine performance by the seat of your pants. When the settings are farther off, fine. You have to give them a go. But repeated fiddling will simply wear the parts out, and sooner or later you will lose a screw or strip a bolt or damage something.

TUNING THE 2-CYCLE

Now that we have explained why you shouldn't fuss with your machine every time it coughs, here is a list of the major tune-up items. Each procedure is described in a previous chapter.

Check the plug(s). Clean, regap, or replace as needed.
Clean the exhaust.
Clean or replace the air filter.
Drain and clean the fuel filter(s).
Decarbonize the upper cylinder.
Clean the reed valve (if there is one).
Replace and gap the contact breaker points.
Adjust ignition timing.
Check carburetor fuel/air mixture and adjust as required.

Check oil injector pump and adjust as required.
Measure the compression of each cylinder.

Note that it is always better to run the fuel/air mixture on the richer side. *Too lean a mix can burn out the engine.*

Note, too, that it is always better to have a little more oil shot into the fuel or into the various lube points rather than a little less, because a shortage of lube can quickly destroy your engine.

TUNING THE 4-CYCLE

Check the plug(s). Clean, regap, or replace as needed.
Clean the exhaust.
Clean or replace the air filter.

Removing the inside of a muffler for cleaning.

Drain and clean the fuel filter(s).
Check valve tappet clearances.
Replace and gap the contact breaker points.
Adjust ignition timing.
Check carburetor fuel/air mixture. Adjust as required.
Measure the compression of each cylinder.

Measurement of compression is not a tune-up procedure, but it will keep you from going out of your calabash should your bike perform no better after tune-up than before.

Note that you are always safer setting the tappets gaps a little wider than narrower. Set too tightly or close, exhaust valves will burn out.

14

Frame Care and Repair

The mark of a serious cyclist is a beautiful bike. It isn't necessarily big and powerful, and it is rarely "way out," with flying handlebars and a step-ladder back. It can be small, light, simple. But it is always bright and shiny, immaculate, a thing of beauty.

KEEPING IT BRIGHT

It would seem that all you need do with a new bike to keep its color bright is to simply keep it out of the rain and clean it when it get dirty. Regrettably, this is not the case. You can quickly dull the finish on your bike by improper cleaning, over-cleaning, and by using the wrong cleaning and polishing agents.

Improper Cleaning. Every time you ride your bike or just leave it outdoors for a spell it gathers dust. If you simply wipe the dust off, you will abrade the paint. The chrome will not be troubled as much because it is hard, but it, too, will be adversely affected to some degree.

It doesn't matter how soft a cloth you may use; dust is an abrasive, and when you wipe it off you abrade the paint and metal. Obviously, if there is a heavy layer of dust and dirt, the effect will be greater. In a short time, energetic dry wiping will dull the best paint job.

Correct Cleaning. The cycle should never be wiped. Should it collect dust and dirt and even thick mud, let them remain until you can *wash* the machine clean. This is best done with a large sponge and a hose. But if you don't have a hose handy, you can use a couple of buckets of water.

Pour the water over the metal. (Never on a hot engine at any time, and not on a cold engine and ignition if you can help it.) You don't need much water, just enough to get the dirt thoroughly wet so you can easily remove it with a gentle touch of the wet sponge.

You do not need soap in the water. Dirt will come off with clear water. If your machine has been in competition and is splattered with oil and grease, use a clean cloth dipped in kerosene (gasoline, if you have nothing better) to remove the oils after you have used the plain water.

To get rid of the oil-solvent residue, you will need soap. Use a little household detergent. It is not advisable to use the soap directly on the oil and grease because they sometimes combine to form a scum that is difficult to remove. In any case, do not use soap where there is no oil present because it tends to dull and to remove the wax that should be on the paint and bright-work.

If you have picked up some road tar, use a soft stick to remove the bulk of it. Follow with a solvent and a series of clean rags. Try to confine your cleaning and wiping to a small area because the tar becomes a stain when dissolved and tends to spread. Remove the tar before washing with soap. You can ignore it a while if you just use cold water.

Preserving the Finish. Wax is the best and simplest means of keeping your paint and metal bright. It is applied only after the paint and chrome are perfectly clean. Do not apply over road tar because the tar will soften and spread.

There is nothing special or tricky about waxing. Just apply a thin coat and rub it to a shine. Once it shines there is nothing but exercise involved in continued rubbing. You *can't* rub it in.

Make certain you use a pure wax. Do not use a wax-cleaner

or a polish-cleaner. Pure wax does not abrade, dissolve, or otherwise remove a layer of paint when you apply it. The others do, and although they have their uses, as will shortly be discussed, wax-cleaners and similar compounds remove paint and should not be used indiscriminately. If you really attack your wheel with a wax-cleaner or a cleaner-polisher every time you should be washing it in plain water, you will go right through your paint job in short order.

You can be certain you are applying wax and nothing else when your application pad does not pick up the color of your bike. When the pad quickly becomes the same color as the paint, you can be certain you are removing paint.

A layer of wax on your paint and chrome protects the paint from the sun's rays, which tend to bleach paint and make the surface of the vehicle shiny and slippery. A waxed surface will not pick up dust and grime as quickly as a bare surface. You will know that you need more wax when you wash the bike and the water lies flat. Water tends to form large globules on a waxed surface.

RESTORING COLOR AND BRIGHTNESS

With time the best formulated and cared-for paint discolors, darkens, bleaches, and fades—all at the same time. The action of the sun removes the oils from the paint. This makes it white. Road oils penetrate the paint, making it darker. With these effects combined, the paint drifts toward a pale gray. At the same time some colors simply disappear. Red, for example, is highly fugitive. As a result, maroon ages into a blue.

The change is skin deep. By using the proper "cleaners" you can remove the top layer of old paint and expose a bright new layer of paint. The trick to getting a good job lies in removing the old paint evenly.

Choice of Paint Cleaners. Depending on how much paint you want to remove, you can use a wax-cleaner, which removes a little at a time; a polish-cleaner, which generally removes more; or a "cutting agent," which removes the most. Most cycle and auto supply shops carry the cutting agents in two grit sizes. The type called "rubbing" compound is the most coarse, while the "polishing" compound is finer because the grit is smaller.

Generally, the rubbing compound is used for removing a faded layer of paint. The paint is washed clean with soap and water. All road tar is removed. The compound is rubbed over the surface of the paint with a clean, damp cloth. As soon as you stop hearing a fine, scratching sound, discard the compound and cloth and start afresh. When the paint surface is evenly bright, you are finished. Wash down with soap and water, dry and repeat with a light touch of polishing compound, then finish with a waxing.

REMOVING DENTS AND BUMPS

It is fairly easy to "bang out" fender or mudguard dents and bumps. Tank dents cannot be brought out, but they can be filled.

Banging out Dents. Remove the part to be straightened, then clean it. Form some pads from old pillows or some plastic foam and clamp the part in a bench vise. You just need enough pressure to hold the metal in place. Borrow or purchase a dolly—a metal block—that fits the curvature of the part. Place the dolly against one side of the metal, and bang gently away on the other side with a metal-working hammer, or any light hammer. Don't attack the central or deep portion of the dent, but work slowly around it, straightening a little of the metal at a time.

Bear in mind that you are flattening the metal between the hammer and the metal block. There is no force or pressure exerted against the vice. In some instances you can even let the part rest on the floor. Never bang the metal without the dolly back-up or you'll make new dents.

When the area is fairly smooth, wash it down with perfectly clean paint thinner, pure turpentine, alcohol, or any clean solvent. Do not use gasoline because it leaves a residue. Use a clean cloth to do the washing and do not touch the metal after you have cleaned it. To make certain the paint sticks, be sure there isn't the slightest trace of oil or grease on the metal or old paint surface. Next, give the part a spray coat of metal primer and let it dry hard.

At this point you may notice that the surface is not perfectly smooth. You have the option of using a file, coarse sandpaper on a block, or a power grinder to take down the high spots or of using putty to fill in the low spots. If it is going to require putty more than ⅛th inch thick, it will be best to go the grind-down route. Better yet, do some more banging.

Assuming you have finished grinding or filing, repeat the wash and primer spray routine. Let it dry hard, and you are ready for the auto putty.

Applying Putty. Use a rubber squeegee made for the purpose. Apply a thin layer, keeping your fingers off the metal. Let the layer dry very hard. If you need more, apply and wait until it has dried. When dry, check the surface, using fine sandpaper on a block of wood.

If there are depressions, fill them in. If you chip paint from the metal, take the primer route again. When you are finished you should have a perfectly smooth surface. If your sandpaper has left scratches, fill them with putty. Let dry and smooth with successively finer grades of sandpaper, ending up with 600 dry. (The higher the number, the finer the paper.)

SPRAY PAINTING

Your fender or frame is now perfectly smooth. There are no visible scratches. All bare metal to be painted has been given a coat of primer and no surface has been touched—if it has, it has been washed clean.

Now you should provide yourself with a clean, dust-free room or area for painting. If you have prepared the metal properly, and if your room is really dust-free, you can do a beautiful job with no more than a few cans of spray paint.

Preparing the Room for Spraying. If you are in a bare basement, hose it down—walls, floor, and ceiling. If you can't hose the room down, vacuum it thoroughly, for if there is any lingering dust in that room it will wind up on your paint job.

Be certain to open all the windows, and don't smoke; paint fumes are explosive.

The room should be warm, perferably around 80° F. You can paint in a cooler room, but if it is much below 70° F you are going to have trouble. The paint will not dry fast enough. The metal to be painted can be warmer than the room's air, but not hot and not much below 70° F.

Choosing the Paint. Three basic types of paint are used for automotive finishing today: lacquer, enamel, and acrylic. Lacquer is easiest to handle. It goes on smoothly and doesn't run (drip) readily. However, it doesn't dry with a shine and it will not hide any scratches. If lacquer is applied to a shiny surface, it will usually shine. Applied to a dull surface, it will be dull.

Enamel dries with a shine. But it dries more slowly, has a tendency to run, and is sensitive to the moisture in the air. It takes considerably more skill to lay down a good spray coat of enamel.

Since acrylic is not readily available in spray cans, we will have to pass it up. It is the most modern paint, but since you can get as good results with the other two paints, it is not too important to our purpose.

If you are not an experienced spray painter, this writer strongly suggests you stick with lacquer and apply the shine with elbow grease. When the paint is hard, give it a couple of warm days, then tackle it with polishing compound. You'll get as good a shine with almost no danger of ruining the job.

Preparing the Paint. If the room in which the paint has been stored for a day or so is warm, the paint is ready to go so soon as you shake it well. If not, place the can in warm water for a half-hour or so.

Applying the Paint. Support the object to be painted so that you are free to ply your art. Protect the areas behind and beneath your wheel or fender or whatever with old papers, because the paint that doesn't reach its target is going to fall down as overspray—dry or semi-dry paint.

Hold the can about ten inches from the target. Press the button with the spray directed to one side. Now, with the spray coming out, sweep past your target. When fully past, release the button. In other words, the paint spray never starts or ends on the object to be painted and the paint spray is always moving.

Watch the work and shift the can to object distance so as to apply a full coat of wet paint—not so much that you drip and not so little (holding the can too far away or moving too fast) that the spray arrives semidry.

With the work piece fully covered, turn the can upside down and press the button until the air coming out of the can is clear. This cleans the nozzle, otherwise it will seal itself solid.

Wait about five minutes, or until the paint is semidry, and then apply the second coat. After the second coat, let the paint dry thoroughly before applying any more coats.

The more coats the better, up to a point. Some owners apply as many as twenty coats and more. Generally the top coats are clear; this gives the paint an appearance of depth.

When you apply more than two or three coats, you must be certain the undercoats are perfectly dry and hard. If they are not, you may trap some of the solvent and the paint may never harden properly. At the same time, it is good to bring the surface of the paint to a shine before you build up too many coats.

To polish the paint you must be certain it is hard, otherwise your grit will chew it up and your work will be wasted. There is no hard-and-fast rule about drying time, but the warmer and dryer the room, and the better its air circulation, the faster the drying will be (Commercial paint shops often bake the finish dry.) Every time you polish you must wash the surface absolutely clean of polish, fingerprints, and grime before you paint again.

METAL CARE

Dull and pitted chrome can be brightened with any of the metal polishes formulated for the purpose. Once bright, a good coat of wax will help keep it so.

However, polish will never bring badly pitted chrome surfaces to new-metal glow. The only sure restorative is replating. The part is removed from the wheels, buffed bright with polishing compound, and brought to a plating outfit. Doing your own buffing will save a few dollars. You'll find platers listed in the local phone book, and some advertise in the cycle magazines.

You can have any piece of metal plated that you wish. But if it isn't smooth and shiny, it will not shine after plating, because the new layer of metal will repeat the surface of the old down to the finest hairline.

Polishing and Buffing. The easy way is by machine. A buffing wheel—discs of sewn cloth made for the purpose—is mounted on a grindstone motor or an electric drill supported in a vise. You start with rubbing compound on rough surfaces. Follow with polish after cleaning the work and the buffer, and finish with jeweler's rouge or some similar polish for the final touch, again cleaning the work and wheel before changing to finer grit.

Working with Aluminum. Bare aluminum can be treated the same way. You polish and buff until you get the shine you want. For additional information on caring for aluminum you might write to The Aluminum Association, 750 Third Avenue, New York, New York 10017.

BENT FRAMES

It all depends on what has been bent and how badly. Some frame parts are replaceable. Others are not. If the bend is slight, you may be able to straighten it by clamping a 2 x 4 to the part to get leverage and getting a hefty friend to sit on the balance of the frame.

If the bend is so bad you get a kink, even as shallow as ⅛ of an inch when you straighten the part, I'd junk it. It has been weakened too much.

CRACKED FRAMES

Cracked frames can be brazed if the crack isn't too long and if some sort of reinforcement in the form of a fish plate

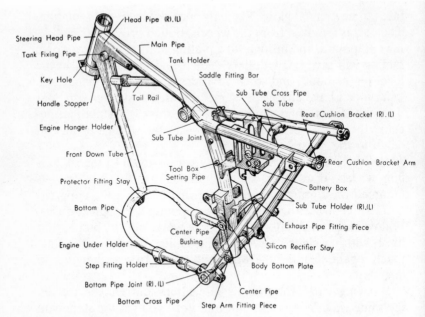

Frame of the Honda 250 Scrambler. *Courtesy Honda*

is used. A fish plate consists of two strips of metal fastened to either side of a joint or break. On a tube you can use two sections of pipe. Have it bronze-brazed. Don't have it welded. Welding will embrittle the metal.

Plastic Parts

Cracked and broken plastic fenders and other frame components can be patched with fiberglass repair kits. The work is simple enough, and if you can hide the patch on the underside of the part, no one will notice the repair. For those fine cracks and even breaks, you might try some of that new cement —the kind that is strong enough to hold a car. It really works, but don't get any between your fingers. You'll tear your skin trying to pry your fingers apart.

15

Touring

The first question about touring concerns the matter of where to go. The quick and pat answer is to say almost anywhere. But not so fast, Lighthorse Harry. No one bike is going to carry you comfortably everywhere. If you are planning on hitting the backwoods trails, you need one type of bike—a trail bike. If you are going to travel our expressways, you are going to require a road bike. If you are hoping to travel both trails and hardtop you must compromise, and the chances are that you will not be satisfied in either circumstance.

Accordingly, your first decision should be concerned with precisely where you wish to tour or travel, and your second decision may well center around how much you want or need to compromise—if you are going to compromise at all. To help you make these decisions, let's review bike requirements for trail and highway travel.

HIGHWAY OR TOURING BIKES

All road bikes must conform to state laws. This means the bike must be capable of keeping up with traffic and must carry proper lights. If you are planning to visit the fifty states or a major portion thereof, you will necessarily be traveling the superhighways.

At this writing the national speed limit is 55 mph, which isn't much at all for a bike. However, few if any bikes are designed to be operated all out for any length of time. If 55 mph is maximum, you will want a bike that is capable of at least 75 mph. First, you don't want the poor machine busting a gut. You want it to be able to *cruise* at 55. That means you must have plenty of horses to spare. Also, there will be hills and head winds. The bike will wear and lose efficiency. You'll require adequate acceleration. All this means extra horses between the wheels.

For riding comfort you will want a fairly heavy bike with a large seat so that you can shift your weight around as you ride to avoid muscular stiffness. A windscreen to protect you from the wind, bugs, and road dust is also a must.

A properly designed screen or shield will not slow you down. In fact, it may even give you a few extra miles because it will reduce your wind resistance. The top of the screen should be just below your comfortable eye level. The screen pushes the wind up and over your head. You don't need it in front of your eyes.

You'll want as many gear changes as you can afford. The more shifts you have the better you will be able to match your engine speed to road conditions. This will improve fuel efficiency.

An extended tail bar with rear lights is also advisable. Other desirable assets include a big single or double headlight up front, plenty of electrical capacity, electric starting so you won't be embarrased should your cycle quit at a light, and a gas tank or tanks large enough to give you better than two hundred miles of cruising distance before you need to refuel.

Most riders select a 4-cycle engine for highway touring because it is smoother and less noisy than a 2-cycle engine. It also throws less exhaust fumes. Gear ratios will be medium to high. Standard tires at recommended tire pressures will be used front and back. The engine will have at least two cylinders, but preferably three or more. It will displace anywhere from 250 to more than 1,000 cc. And it will weigh, fully loaded, from 400 to more than 1,000 pounds.

To summarize: the road touring machine is big, heavy, and sassy. It is going to haul you and your friend and luggage several hundred miles a day. It has to be big and powerful to do so and not shake you to jelly in the process.

TRAIL BIKES

A trail is an unpaved road. It may be wide enough for two cars to pass. It may be hard and fairly smooth. Then again, it may be little more than a goat's footpath—bumpy, rocky, and filled with more twists and curves than a Moorish belly dancer in action.

Unless you stick to the hard, wide, dirt roads, you'll find the big tour bike a real drag. You won't be able to guide it around the corners the way you wish. You won't be able to "horse" it up hills, around obstacles, through water, over rocks, and fallen trees. If your big bike flops, you are going to need a crew to help you lift it up.

For trail riding you need a bike that you can "manhandle." For most of us this means a bike that weighs less than 200 pounds when fully loaded—without the rider aboard. The less

A bike loaded and ready for a trip. *Courtesy American Motorcycle Association*

the bike weighs—all things being equal—the easier it will be for you to control the bike on a bad trail.

To get the most power for the weight, you will probably choose a 2-cycle, single-cylinder engine. Its displacement will probably be around 100 cc, but it is difficult to put a limit on displacement. The better the machine or engine, the less it will weigh and the more horsepower it will develop.

You'll want a low-to-medium range of engine-to-rear-wheel gear ratios. You'll no doubt use knobby tires on the rear wheel and you'll run it fairly soft. This means it is absolutely essential to have tire clinchers on both wheels.

You'll also be wise to select a bike with a fairly high "belly" clearance so that there is less of a chance of the engine getting hung up on an obstruction. The ignition system should be thoroughly waterproofed—there are sprays you can apply—and the tail pipe should be fairly high so that it is not under water when you ford a stream.

Spray a waterproof compound on your electrical and ignition components to keep them from being plagued by water. This is an ignition coil mounted high on the frame.

Some of the trail riders run without mudguard or modified guards, but it is advisable to have them because the wheels can kick up a lot of mud and dirt.

Because you will not ride at night—nighttime trail riding can be suicide—you will not need more than a minimum electrical system. The tour bike, by contrast, needs a maximum electrical system because you may be riding the highways after dark.

Trail Bike Modifications. With experience you will no doubt work up your own list of bike changes, and very possibly some of the following suggestions may differ from yours. No matter, here is what some of the trail riders are doing and the reasons why.

To save weight, all the flash is removed. Everything that isn't vital to the operation of the bike is taken off and stored for the time the bike may be offered for resale. For additional weight reduction the standard rims and hubs are replaced with aluminum rims and hubs. The tach and speedometer are removed.

To prevent severing of a leg artery and/or equally important parts, all obstructions behind the driver are removed or covered in some fashion. The reason is that all trail riders fall off their bikes—usually by slipping off backwards. It's part of the fun or hazard of the game—take your pick.

When you are running your 2-cycle on the trails, you should cut the idling speed as far down as you can without being troubled by engine stalling. A 2-cycle engine has very little braking power. If it has been set at normal idle, say 1,200 rpm, you will race down any hill unless you apply the brakes. Reducing the idling speed gets some braking action out of the 2-cycle engine.

At the same time, it is advisable to enrich the idling gas mixture. This insures the engine plenty of lube at idling—2-strokers not point-lubricated depend on oil in the fuel for lubrication—and also helps prevent the engine from stumbling when you give it the throttle. If you try to quickly rev up a slowly idling engine with a standard or normal fuel/air mixture, the engine will hesitate and often stall.

If the bike comes with a wide pair of handlebars, you should switch to a narrower pair so that there is less chance to get hung up in the bushes. The grips themselves should be horizontal. If they point down there is a tendency for your hands to slip off.

Should you plan to ride very rough trails, you might want to install a skid plate of aluminum beneath the bike's belly. It only adds a couple of pounds and it can save the engine in the event you hit a rock.

PLANNING THE TRIP

Some of us don't like to plan. It's too constricting. We like the freedom of just hopping aboard and taking off whenever the mood strikes. This is lovely when you are lucky and everything turns out fine. But why depend on luck? You can travel any road in the country and miss a thousand interesting things to see and do simply because you do not know they exist or they are taking place just out of sight. You can get into all sorts of needless trouble simply because you didn't take the time necessary to plan and prepare.

Where and When. To some degree these two decisions are inseparable. You go when you can go, of course. But the season of the year will or should, to some extent, determine where you go. Obviously it is foolish to head for the far north when winter is coming up, and almost as incautious to head for the deep south when summer is upon us.

Not so obvious are the refinements of these decisions. For example a northbound trip just before winter takes hold is ideal for the deep woods and Canadian territories. This is the time of late Indian summer when all the bugs have quieted down. So long as you scoot before the snow flies, you'll enjoy all the pleasures of the north woods and none of the problems.

Midsummer is fine for the high ground. Remember, your bike can take you up into the sky for several miles. If you go to Mexico City, for example, you'll be nearly 2½ miles up. This is the time to explore the mountains of Colorado and New Mexico or the high plateaus of Wyoming and Montana.

Honda 500 being used on a tour of back roads in the Rockies. *Courtesy American Motorcycle Association*

Within the broad areas just sketched out lie many smaller local variations. For example, the coastal areas, even up north, offer mild weather almost through December, yet twenty miles inland there may be snow. Our central plains have very short spells of what most of us would call good or even acceptable weather. The summers run over 100° F, the winters go below zero, and every now and again a tornado stirs things up.

Therefore, where you go will be determined to a great extent by when you go. The bike isn't an all-weather machine, though you can hard-head it through most of the muck if you are really determined. But it's not fun.

Close-up view of a bike on well-paved highway protected by guard rails in the Rockies. *Courtesy American Motorcycle Association*

Maps and Data. Most gasoline service stations will provide you with all the main and secondary road maps you will need. If they can't do it, you can write to the major oil companies or the AAA. Maps and data on the back roads and trails are the items that will be hard to come by. There are any number of published books devoted to public camping grounds. They offer some information.

You can write to the American Motorcycle Association, P.O. Box 141, Westerville, Ohio 43081, for whatever they may have, including the names and addresses of motorcycle trail-riding clubs near your area of interest. These clubs may have the "poop" you need.

You can also write to the U.S. Geological Survey, Washington, D.C., or Denver, Colorado. They publish a very fine comprehensive set of detailed maps. In fact, they are so detailed that you first ask for an index of the state or states of interest, and then you select the sectional map or maps of the area you are going to explore. At last check each sheet cost approximately fifty cents.

As for things to see, points of historical and geographical interest, write to the department of parks and recreation of each state. Address the Commissioner; don't fool with the little fry. Generally, they are located in the state's capital. Many of the larger cities also have park and recreation departments that offer free literature concerning their city's attractions.

Select Your Companions Carefully. There is an old Indian saying that advises—you don't know a teepee until you have slept in it. Well, you don't know a bike companion until you have ridden with him or her for several days. Your companions may be all that you could wish for on the ball field, on the racetrack, or even by your side on the job. But out on the road they may disappoint you, and by the same token, you may disappoint them, without either of you doing anything wrong. Be advised that the smaller the group the more likely there will be friction. When there are five or six riders, a lot of small compromises are constantly made. When it's a head-to-head condition, it is no longer a compromise but a major concession.

Since there always has to be a first time for any traveling group, you must expect to encounter these situations, but you can reduce the risk by *agreeing well beforehand* about everything you are planning to do.

You should decide how fast you will ride, how many hours to stay in the saddle, when and where you will stop for grub, how much food and what food you will bring—even how many minutes will be spent watching the waterfalls or other scenic attractions.

It may sound childish, but you just can't sit down to a steak you have broiled to perfection over the fire while your chosen companion opens a can of beans. He didn't bring anything else because he didn't want to bother cooking. He has to be superhuman to eat his cold beans with relish and not stare hungry-eyed at your steak.

Some years ago a friend and I went partners on a car though we were told the partnership would end in an argument. We fooled everyone by agreeing and adhering to a rigid schedule. We divided the week into alternate days beginning at 6:00 A.M. On *my* days the car was all mine. I could do anything I wished with it. I didn't have to drive it if I didn't want to. I didn't even have to let him in the car, if I didn't feel so inclined. The car was mine. On his days it was all his.

Before you ride off into the sunset, decide on such unexpected but not impossible things as a complete bike breakdown. What do you do? Do you all go home? Do you ship his bike home and have him ride double? (I wouldn't want anyone except a pretty girl riding behind me for two or three weeks.) If so, who gets him? Or does he take his lumps like a gentleman and go home with his bike—or hang around a lonely repair shop by himself and catch up as best he can?

Another, more likely problem that may arise to plague you is money. How much should you bring? How much do you allot for food and lodgings? Will it be greasy spoons and guest houses or luxury restaurants and plush motels? Will it be sleeping under the stars or in town under sheets?

All these points and more should be thrashed out well in advance of take-off time. Agreements reached beforehand can prevent an awful lot of bickering and discontent after you've begun your trip.

Mileage. On an open road you shouldn't figure on going more than 400 miles each day. Not that you cannot do more on a heavy machine, but the danger of mishaps—a nice word for a bloody spill and road burn—increases with fatigue. Also, don't ride at twilight or at night if you can help it. Of the two, twilight is the worst. There is a lot of sky light at this time with comparatively little ground light. Vision is reduced because one's pupils contract in response to the light coming down from the sky. As a result, your ability and that of others

Yamaha trail bike parked near scenic spot along New England coastline.
Courtesy American Motorcycle Association

A wayside stop under trees with cold well water at hand is a welcome respite on a summer afternoon. *Courtesy American Motorcycle Association*

to distinguish objects on the ground is greatly reduced. This time of day is responsible for the highest incidence of traffic accidents.

Another point is that if you are riding to merely cover ground, you are missing much of the purpose of bike touring—which is to see and explore and to meet new people. If all you do is sit your wheels, you aren't going to see much more than the roadside.

What to Bring Along

Part of the fun of traveling is deciding on what you are going to take along. It is a kind of a game in which you try to anticipate all your needs while keeping your baggage as limited as possible.

Tools and Parts. At the very least, I'd include a crescent wrench to handle the readily accessible nuts and bolts; other wrenches to handle those the crescent can't fit or reach; screwdrivers, gas pliers, vise grips, a chain breaker, and tire irons. As for parts and things, I'd include a tire patch kit, several tiny metal bottles of CO_2, an adapter, spare plug, some lengths of electrical wire, baling wire, lots of rubber tape and adhesive tape, a small grease gun or other means for lubricating the chain, spare chain links and pins, spare light bulbs, fuses, and some extra engine oil.

If you are traveling with a group, you can share some of these tools and so reduce the weight. In addition, one of you might carry some 30 feet of ¾-inch manila rope to use for towing. The line is tied high on the lead bike and wrapped twice around the handlebars of the towed bike. The second driver holds the end of the rope. In trouble, he simply lets it go. The second rider keeps tension on the rope, which should have some strips of white or red cloth tied to it so no fool can or will try to go between the cycles. The arrangement is safe enough if there is no traffic and you travel slowly.

Camping Gear. If you are going to rough it, which is an erroneous phrase—because if you know what you are doing, camping can be more comfortable than an air-conditioned

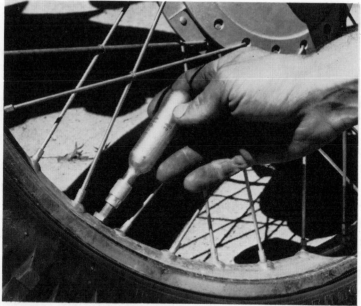

A tiny CO_2 cartridge and adaptor can save you miles of pushing or walking. Single cartridge inflates a tire about half full.

house with an indoor swimming pool—you'll need a tent, sleeping bag, and air mattress for inclement weather and possibly just a bag and mattress for mild weather in insect-free territory.

When you obtain your air mattress, spend a few more bucks and buy a rubber-treated cloth type. The plastic types, while much cheaper, don't last as long. You can dispense with the air mattress if you're sleeping on sand or have a hard backside. If not, and you carry extra blankets to fold beneath you, you'll be carrying much more weight and not gaining very much in insulation.

Get the better bag—the kind with poplin or any of the other finely woven, water-proofed cloth tops. The rubber or plastic bags are no good. You'll sweat to death in them. The quart or so of moisture you exude during the night will have no place to go and you'll wake up soaking wet. The down-filled bag is lightest and warmest, but the Dacron-filled bag is about 75 percent as warm for an equal amount of filler. And get yourself or make an inner liner of cotton that you can have washed. Don't sleep directly on the bag itself if you can help it.

If conditions permit, you can spread your bag on a ground sheet—any waterproof material about six by eight feet—and rig a little shelter just over your head in case of rain.

Don't waste your money on any of the left-over World War I or II pup tents. They aren't fit for a dog. Get yourself a modern mountain tent with a sewn-in floor and at least one, but preferably two screened openings. If you don't mind wrig-

Some trail riders apply masking tape to their gas tanks to reduce the amount of scuffing they get and to give them a better gripping surface for their needs.

gling to get into your bag, the one-man tent should serve you very well.

If you expect to spend time in your tent reading or just sitting up, then purchase the two-man tent. For anything else, there are many designs available. One of the more useful for bike camping is the Draw-Tie tent used by Admiral Byrd on his South Pole expedition. It has all its poles on the outside, which leaves more room for people and other creatures on the inside.

Looking at the prices for these things—and you can easily drop two bills for the tent, bag, and mattress alone—you might wonder why you should get almost the best (the best is beyond our reach—it's the kind of gear that goes to the top of Mount Everest), and not try to save a few dollars on the equipment. You may figure it isn't important, but it is. This is where you are going to live. If you can't sit out the rain comfortably in your tent, if you don't sleep dry and comfortably you are going to be miserable the following morning and may wind up getting sick.

So get into that sleeping bag before you purchase it. Set up that tent and try it for size and ease of erection and packing. Select gear with an eye to keeping it for years. Good camping equipment can last a long, long time.

Cooking Equipment. If you aren't good at building fires quickly—and in some parks in certain seasons you aren't allowed to build an open fire—bring along a stove. The best and lightest are the Primus types. But they are also the most expensive. The propane types give plenty of cooking heat, but you have the bulk of the stove and the nuisance of the gas cartridges.

If you are traveling alone and don't mind fussing with your food, a single burner will suffice. But to really get a meal going in a hurry you need two burners. It must be large enough to heat a quart of water to boiling in about fifteen minutes at the most. If there is a gang, you'll need several stoves.

Generally speaking, however, cooking equipment requirements are surprisingly few. You can heat soup in a frypan. You can make water for coffee in a deep saucepan, preferably with a cover so it will heat more quickly. You'll find nesting sets of pots and pans for one, two, and more people in the sport shops and Army-Navy stores. They are reasonably priced and very convenient, but don't fail to bring along a large, heavy porcelain cup for coffee or tea. You'll burn your lip trying to drink hot liquid from an aluminum cup.

And don't forget pot-cleaning equipment. Those S.O.S. scrubbing pads are fine. Also, bring along paper towels for wiping the dishes and general cleanup, and large plastic garbage bags for sealing up the garbage every night so you don't attract new friends. For water at the campsite you will find a canvas bucket just dandy. It is porous, which lets the water evaporate and cool itself. For riding you'll need a canteen. Its size will depend on where you are. In the desert a walking man needs several gallons of water a day to survive. In the winter a couple of quarts is more than enough. So use your judgment.

Your problem will be how to mount the canteen on the bike in such fashion as to keep it perfectly fixed. If it vibrates it may knock or wear a hole through its wall. My suggestion is that you cut an old inner tube into rings and use them to lash the can in place.

Food. There has been a tremendous development in dried and compressed and otherwise specially treated foods in the past few years. There is almost nothing you cannot purchase in condensed form. In fact, you can even buy dried ice cream. (I don't know how the dried ice cream tastes, but I can assure you that the dried cheese omelet is delicious.) These foods are expensive but they do save weight, and it's wise to carry some packages along for emergencies—when you haven't time and conditions aren't propitious for making a regular meal.

There are also the old camping standbys such as regular Quaker Oats, to which you can add raisins; salami, which can stand the heat without refrigeration; and hard cheese, which does fairly well in the heat if it's kept airtight. To these staples you can add local produce and fresh meats and fish so that you have variety without carrying a grocery bag on your back wheel.

Packaging. The cartons and cans in which most foods are

packaged can pose problems. The simplest and, for me anyway, best way of handling these things is to repack them in plastic bags. Use them double or triple and tie them with their wires. By doing so you can get a lot of loose foods such as sugar and cereal into a mighty small space.

RIDING TRAILS

While the subject of riding trails deserves a book in its own right, we shall endeavor to cram as much information as possible into the space available.

No matter how well you may know a particular trail, it remains an unpaved road. Woodland creatures are apt to burrow into it, leaving soft spots and holes for the unfortunate. Trees and tree branches often fall across it. Rocks and stones may roll down upon it. A spring freshet may soak a portion. In the late fall and very early spring sections may be covered with hoar frost, glaze ice, even snow. The sunny section of the trail may be perfectly dry and hard, yet round the bend in the shadows the ice or water remains.

The previous paragraph by no means lists all the changes that occur daily on the trails—just the ones that come quickly to mind. In addition, remember that unless you are riding on private property, others are also using the trails. They may be on horse, foot, bicycle, or another motorcycle. They may even be in a jeep or bush buggy. The sound of your bike can easily hide the sound of their approach. So you must constantly watch the blind turns.

SAFETY TIPS

Practice Does It. The trick to deep-woods cycling safety and even pleasure is learning how to handle the bike up and down hills and on all kinds of surfaces. The way to learn safety is to ride these surfaces on the flats, where there are no additional obstacles and there is plenty of room for error.

Stopping. Find yourself a nice soft, broad, unused stretch of level dirt. Start with speeds of about 20 mph and make a series of quick stops, increasing your speed a little each time and using nothing but the rear binder (brake) each time. As you stop from higher speeds, you will hit the skid point. When you do, try it again, but this time tilt your bike a little to your left (or right if you wish) and as you start your skid clamp up more tightly on the brake. You want your bike to cock a little and go into a controlled, limited slide. You will stop a little faster this way and you won't be surprised at the direction in which the rear end skids.

In other words, it is impossible to prevent skidding during an emergency stop on a loose dirt road, so you want to learn how to control the skid. In a way, you bring the bike to a stop somewhat the same way you make a side stop when ice skating.

With serious effort you will be able to do this at 30 or even 40 mph with no sweat. When you get to that expert level, try gently applying the front brake, starting once again with a lower speed. Dual braking will, of course, give you a faster stop, but if you're not careful the first time, you may also learn to fly.

Turns. Once you have learned to make a proper skid stop, repeat the exercise at a low speed, but instead of coming to a full stop, give your bike the throttle as you slow down and get your backside to point in the right direction. You don't need this at normal trail speeds on fairly firm dirt, but should you meet trouble it is well to have the confidence and ability to pull out in a hurry.

Keep Your Feet on the Pegs. Don't drag your feet just to rest them. Don't plant them when going round turns or stopping. You're not on asphalt and anything can stub your toe—at which instant, if it is in front of the foot peg, you will break your leg. You don't use your feet, no matter how big and flat they may be, to make a turn.

Bumps. You can take the pain out of your rear end by standing up on the pegs when the road gets really bad or you see a bump ahead. Your knees can take the shock better than other parts of your anatomy, and getting the weight rearward helps the front end come up. For a big bad one, give the engine a shot and do a wheelie, if you can.

Muck and Mire. So long as you can keep moving, you are all right. So don't slow down. Should you have to down gear, shift as fast as you can. The moment your front wheel sinks in is the moment you stop. Standing up and moving your weight rearward helps to lift the front and increase your traction.

Downhill. There are two dangers in this situation: one, that your bike will accelerate more quickly than you can take measures to stop it; and, two, that you may panic. The second is much more dangerous.

Fear of falling is basic to all of us, and it is not unnatural to experience goose pimples looking down a steep hill. But this is a fear you can learn to control, and the way to do it is by starting with gentle hills and working your way up by taking them a little faster each time until you know you can handle your bike.

During this training period remember, don't ever put your feet on the ground. There is a tremendous desire in all of us to do this as we zoom downhill, but this is the best time to break a leg by catching a toe. So keep your feet on the pegs.

Start by using your rear brake only. Learn to balance the bike coming down very slowly so that on a really steep hill you can do the same. To save your brake on a long, steep descent, shift into low gear and, if necessary, cut the engine.

Some riders walk their bikes down steep hills, but I believe you are safer in the saddle, both brakes almost locked, creeping down the hill than walking beside the bike, front brake locked, trying to keep the rear of the bike from dragging you down.

Tilt. When the road is canted along the side of a hill, you have to stand up on the pegs and tilt the bike away from the high side of the road while you lean toward the opposite side to balance it.

Riding Comfort. When you have learned to handle dirt turns, stops, and hills, you will sit your bike more easily and you will be able to relax somewhat. You won't be fighting the bike. It will take a little time but eventually you will find dirt and trail bike riding no more of a strain than hardtop motorcycling.

16

Safety Review

As we stated in the first chapter of this book, it is the beginning cyclist who suffers most of the injuries and fatalities that occur to motorcyclists as a group, and these usually take place during his or her first 500 miles of riding.

More than 90 percent of all the bike fatalities are the result of head injuries. And if we study all road accidents involving motorcycles, 90 percent of them occur at a highway entrance or exit or an intersection. Few riders fall off their bikes on a highway all by themselves. Those who do rarely injure themselves fatally. Most of the automobile/cycle accidents are caused by automobiles suddenly turning into the path of a motorcycle.

As these facts are stated, they may not appear to have much significance. They are statistics—no more, no less. If, however, you are more than slightly interested in maintaining your health and, in fact, your life, it will repay you considerably to invest some time in memorizing the following points.

Don't ride without a helmet.
Keep clear of automobiles and watch out for their blind spots.

Keep clear of big trucks—they can see even less to their sides and rear than motorists.

Be doubly careful on highway approaches and exits.

Be extra cautious at intersections and when emerging from side streets or roads.

Drive slowly and carefully when you are learning; stay off the highways, out of the narrow back streets.

Be especially careful at dusk—that's when most accidents occur.

Don't ride when you are very tired, or have had a couple of drinks. Remember, it takes the average body about an hour to rid itself of one ounce of 90 proof alcohol.

Don't ride when your cycle isn't in top condition.

Avoid riding at night if you possibly can.

Index